COOL NAMES

for Babies

· · ·

COOL NAMES

for Babies

. . .

Pamela Redmond Satran

and

Linda Rosenkrantz

ST. MARTIN'S GRIFFIN

NEW YORK

www.stmartins.com

BOOK DESIGN BY AMANDA DEWEY

Library of Congress Cataloging-in-Publication Data

Satran, Pamela Redmond.
    Cool names for babies / Pamela Redmond Satran and Linda Rosenkrantz.—1st. ed.
        p. cm.
    ISBN 0-312-30439-0
    1. Names, Personal—Dictionaries. I. Rosenkrantz, Linda. II. Title.

CS2377.S38 2003
929.4'4—dc21

                                    2003043113

First Edition: August 2003

10 9 8 7 6 5 4 3 2 1

Contents

II. COOL COOL—Famous Names · 53

III. PRE-COOL COOL—Old Names · 109

IV. NEW COOL—Creative Names · 131

Introduction

We got the idea for this book when we were doing publicity for our last book on names, *Baby Names Now*. One after another, interviewers seemed to ask us the same question, "What are the cool names?" And each time, we found ourselves stumped.

Since we wrote our first book together, *Beyond Jennifer & Jason* (now amended to *Beyond Jennifer & Jason, Madison & Montana*), we've broken down names into the trendy and the classic, the feminine and the androgynous, into categories ranging from Irish to unusual, from Shakespeare to soap opera. Over fifteen years of updates to that book, we'd classified names every way possible except one. We'd never examined precisely what makes a name cool, and which names fit the bill. Of course, we'd spent the last fifteen years thinking about cool names. . . .

And that's the big question today, after all, the thing that most parents—along with those persistent interviewers—want to know. What are the cool names? And how can I choose one for my child?

In examining the issue of cool and names, we reached a few conclusions.

Cool, for the Most Part, Means Unusual.

Cool names today usually are those that are not familiar. Traditional choices like John and Elizabeth (this is undoubtedly the only name book on the market that does not include the names John and Elizabeth—or Michael, Hannah, Jacob, etc.) are simply too normal to be considered cool. And popular favorites like Tyler and Mikayla are too widespread to be cool. Now that the Top Ten names include such once-wild choices as Madison and Alexis, you have to go pretty far beyond the mainstream to find names that are truly cool.

Cool Knows No Boundaries.

All names from all cultures are fair game for American parents in search of cool these days—as well as surnames, place names, nature and day names, transgender names, and word names. And why stop there? In this book, we offer up some new categories no one ever thought of before: foreign-word names, for instance, like Vrai.

If You Can't Find a Cool Name You Like, Make One Up.

Unusual doesn't go far enough for some parents: They want a name that's truly one-of-a-kind. Parents in search of a cool name are more often creating one of their own, and we include here advice on how to do that. Our only caveat: If you want a name that's truly cool, be creative in your invention and don't make a very minor alteration to a very popular name.

There's Plenty of Inspiration Out There for Cool.

The world is full of inspiration for cool baby-naming—and more full every day, thanks to the cool names of characters in movies and books and to the names of celebrities themselves. Plus, with last names now as fair game as first names, the pool of famous names virtually doubles—Madonna and Cher notwithstanding.

Kids Today Are Comfortable with Cool.

When we were growing up, if you had a name like Sonata or Sawyer, other kids thought you were weird. But now that the concept of cool permeates the culture, down to children's own ideas about desirability, kids take unusual names in stride and even admire them. Our own children's friends include an Ash and a Dash, a (boy) Robin and a (girl) Baldwin, a Miles and an Allegra and a Lex and a Xan, and they don't even blink. So if the only thing that's stopping you from choosing a cooler name is worrying about how your child will handle it, don't.

There Are Many Kinds of Cool.

A cool name can be an invented one—or a name from the Bible such as Moses or Tabitha that's fallen out of favor. It can be an androgynous choice like O'Hara, or a name with clear gender associations: Felicity, say, or Finn. Cool names include the earthly (Tierra) and the otherworldly (Jupiter), the ancient (Abel) and the newly minted (Arley). You can find a cool name to suit any sensibility.

Cool Isn't Everything.

Along with many varieties, there are several levels of cool, from the Hot—these are popular names such as Isabella and Isaiah that are widely considered cool—to the Over-the-Top. How far you want to go depends on your taste, your sense of adventure, and where you live. One Manhattan-based parent we know, for instance, recently rejected the name Oscar as "too common"—though in most parts of the country, Oscar is too cool for consideration. So what if you're one of those people who realize you don't want to go even halfway to Oscar? What if you read this book and find yourself intrigued, entertained, inspired . . . and in the end a lot more convinced than you realized that you want to give your child a plain, solid, and decidedly uncool name like John or Elizabeth?

So what indeed. A name is not your personal style statement, a choice with which to impress the world. Rather, you should think of it as something that will identify your child for the rest of his life, a label she will have to live with forever. You may decide that cool is a desirable component of such a lifelong imprimatur. And then again, you may decide that, when it comes to a name, you want nothing to do with cool (just know you well may have to suffer the consequences when your child is a teenager).

And that's fine. But you still owe it to your baby and your choice of a name to read this book. For one thing, we offer hundreds and hundreds of naming options here that you won't find ANYWHERE else. We'll open your eyes to a way of thinking about names that no other book, no other source can. And you'll know for certain, after reading this book, what makes for a cool name—even if you decide that uncool is cool enough for you.

I. HOT COOL

...

Mainstream Names

Dakota

Top 100 of Cool

Many of the names commonly acknowledged as cool are in fact widely used. With Madison at Number 2 on the girls' popularity list—there were nearly 22,000 Madisons born in 2001—such once-offbeat choices as Elijah and Bailey can't be far behind. Here, we go down the most recent Most Popular list from the Social Security office and rank the top cool names.

Depending on your personal tolerance for cool, you may see the names here as either outrageous or a big yawn. In either case, for first-time parents this list may be an eye-opening look at just how popular these choices are. To give you a real-numbers idea of volume, there were just about 5,000 girls born in one recent year named Kylie or Kylee (we didn't even count the Kyleigh's, etc.)—that's nearly 100 in every state. And for those who want to find a name that's cool without being unique or unusual or wild, the names on this list can offer a good compromise.

A note on our methods: We combined spellings, so that some names—Ariana et al., for instance—catapult far up the list. When we include more than one spelling, we list them in order of frequency. Noted here is each name's standing on the Cool Top 100, as well as, in parentheses, its rank on the most recent conventional Popularity List. And while cool is a subjective quality, prompting many differences of opinion even between the two of us, for the most part we excluded classic names such as Michael and Sarah as well as older, perhaps once-cool but now overexposed favorites such as Joshua and Ashley. Any parent who wants to search the national list of top baby names and make their own decisions about which are cool can find the top thousand on-line at http://www.ssa.gov/OACT/babynames.

Girls

1. **ALEXIS** (5)
2. **ABIGAIL** (8)
3. **OLIVIA** (11)
4. **EMMA** (13)
5. **JASMINE/JASMINE/ JAZMIN** (17)
6. **MACKENZIE/MCKENZIE/ MAKENZIE** (18)

7. ANNA (19)
8. DESTINY (22)
9. SYDNEY (23)
10. JULIA (27)
11. ISABELLA (28)
12. MORGAN (29)
13. GRACE (16)
14. CHLOE (30)
15. NATALIE (32)
16. SAVANNAH/SAVANNA (33)
17. MADELINE/MADELYN (34)
18. SOPHIA/SÓFIA (38)
19. GABRIELLA/GABRIELA (43)
20. ARIANA/ARIANNA (44)
21. ISABEL/ISABELLE (45)
22. SIERRA/CIERRA (46)
23. JENNA (48)
24. JORDAN (49)
25. GABRIELLE (50)
26. FAITH (53)
27. MAYA/MYA (47)
28. KYLIE/KYLEE (60)
29. AALIYAH/ALIYAH (63)
30. ZOE (64)
31. TRINITY (67)
32. RILEY/RYLEE (68)
33. BAILEY (70)

34. AUTUMN (73)
35. JADA (75)
36. MIA (77)
37. ALEXA (78)
38. JULIANA/JULIANNA (79)
39. PAYTON/PEYTON (80)
40. CLAIRE (82)
41. MARIAH (86)
42. SKYLAR/SKYLER (90)
43. KYLIE (93)
44. JADE (98)
45. LILY (103)
46. ANGEL (109)
47. SABRINA (113)
48. AUDREY (114)
49. ADRIANA (116)
50. CAMRYN/CAMERON (120)
51. CHEYENNE (121)
52. JILLIAN (123)
53. JOCELYN (124)
54. MIRANDA (130)
55. ALICIA (131)
56. ANGELICA (133)
57. AVA (135)
58. KIARA (136)
59. KENNEDY (140)
60. DAISY (142)
61. NATALIA (145)

62. **ALEXIA** (146)

63. **SUMMER** (147)

64. **SOPHIE** (151)

65. **HOPE** (153)

66. **AVERY** (154)

67. **BIANCA** (155)

68. **VERONICA** (157)

69. **KARINA** (161)

70. **ASHLYN** (162)

71. **BETHANY** (165)

72. **DIAMOND** (170)

73. **BROOKLYN** (174)

74. **GENESIS** (180)

75. **GIANNA** (189)

76. **PAOLA** (194)

77. **ELLA** (195)

78. **MCKENNA** (197)

79. **ARIEL** (201)

80. **AMELIA** (203)

81. **CLAUDIA** (205)

82. **DELANEY** (208)

83. **KYRA** (210)

84. **KENDALL** (211)

85. **AUBREY** (213)

86. **SELENA** (218)

87. **SADIE** (221)

88. **REAGAN** (223)

89. **CHARLOTTE** (230)

90. **RUBY** (235)

91. **RAVEN** (236)

92. **TATIANA** (242)

93. **MACY** (245)

94. **ASIA** (256)

95. **CAROLINA** (257)

96. **JOSEPHINE** (271)

97. **ADDISON** (274)

98. **CELESTE** (287)

99. **MERCEDES** (291)

100. **INDIA** (298)

Boys

1. **TYLER** (13)

2. **DYLAN/DILLON** (21, 176)

3. **CHRISTIAN/CRISTIAN** (24, 146)

4. **ZACHARY** (16)

5. **ETHAN** (17)

6. **BRANDON** (18)

7. **JUSTIN** (22)

8. **AUSTIN** (25)

9. **SAMUEL** (26)

10. **CALEB/KALEB** (38, 116)

11. **NOAH** (28)

12. **LOGAN** (31)

13. NATHAN (33)
14. CAMERON (35)
15. HUNTER (36)
16. GABRIEL (37)
17. JORDAN (39)
18. KYLE (40)
19. AARON (42)
20. DEVIN/DEVON (71, 150)
21. ISAIAH (45)
22. ELIJAH (47)
23. ISAAC (48)
24. JACK (49)
25. CONNOR (50)
26. LUKE (51)
27. MASON (56)
28. EVAN (59)
29. JACKSON (60)
30. NATHANIEL (64)
31. CODY (65)
32. JARED (67)
33. IAN (69)
34. JADEN/JAYDEN (114)
35. COLIN/COLLIN (125, 140)
36. COLE (74)
37. ADRIAN (75)
38. TREVOR (76)
39. BLAKE (77)
40. SEBASTIAN (78)

41. GAVIN (79)
42. CHASE (80)
43. GARRETT (81)
44. JULIAN (82)
45. LUCAS (83)
46. AIDAN (88)
47. JALEN/JAYLEN (127)
48. JESSE (90)
49. JEREMIAH (91)
50. BRYCE (93)
51. XAVIER (95)
52. BRAYDEN/BRADEN
     (177, 194)
53. DAKOTA (96)
54. CARSON (97)
55. DALTON (98)
56. COLBY (99)
57. TANNER (101)
58. SPENCER (102)
59. MARCUS (105)
60. RILEY (106)
61. DOMINIC (107)
62. WYATT (108)
63. TRISTAN (109)
64. CARTER (112)
65. PEYTON/PAYTON (171)
66. BRENDAN (115)
67. OSCAR (117)

68. **HAYDEN** (118)

69. **COLTON** (120)

70. **HENRY** (123)

71. **PARKER** (124)

72. **MAXWELL** (126)

73. **DEREK** (128)

74. **SHANE** (129)

75. **LIAM** (133)

76. **OWEN** (134)

77. **TRAVIS** (137)

78. **GRANT** (138)

79. **ALEXIS** (139)

80. **OMAR** (145)

81. **GAGE** (148)

82. **PRESTON** (154)

83. **DUSTIN** (161)

84. **MAX** (162)

85. **CLAYTON** (164)

86. **TAYLOR** (165)

87. **JOSIAH** (170)

88. **ALEC** (173)

89. **BRADY** (175)

90. **LEVI** (179)

91. **NOLAN** (181)

92. **TRENTON** (182)

93. **MICAH** (183)

94. **DAWSON** (188)

95. **DAMIAN** (190)

96. **GIOVANNI** (195)

97. **CADEN** (196)

98. **CADE** (202)

99. **COOPER** (205)

100. **CHANDLER** (207)

Dolly Molly Polly

Coolator

*O*ften, it doesn't take much to change the cool status of a name. For many girls' names, all you have to do, figuratively, is add an 'a' to the end to bump them up several coolness levels: Joanne to Joanna, Susan to Susanna—you get the picture. The point is that with a bit of ingenuity you can ramp up a name you like to a similar one that's cooler, or tone it down if you want to go in a quieter direction. Here, some examples:

Girls

UNCOOL	COOL	COOLER
ANNE	ANNA	ANYA
BRIANNA	BRYN	BRYONY
CAROL	CAROLINE	CAROLINA
CASEY	CASSIDY	CASSANDRA
CHARLENE	CHARLOTTE	CARLOTTA
CINDY	SYDNEY	SIDONY
CRYSTAL	JADE	RUBY
DAWN	AURORA	ANDROMEDA
DIANE	DIANA	DINAH
DOLLY	MOLLY	POLLY
DORA	NORA	ISADORA
EVELYN	EVE	AVA
FLORIDA	SAVANNAH	LOUISIANA
GENA	GENEVIEVE	GENEVA
GEORGETTE	GEORGIA	GEORGINA
GWEN	GWYNNE	GWYNETH
HEATHER	DAISY	VIOLET
HELENE	HELEN	HELENA
IVANA	IVORY	IVY
JAMIE	JAMES	JAMAICA
JAN	JANNA	JANE
JEANETTE	JENNA	GEMMA
JULIE	JULIA	JULIET

JOAN	JUNE	JUNO
JOANNE	JOANNA	JOSEPHINE
LILIAN	LILY	LILLIALE
LISA	LIZA	ELIZA
LORI	LAURA	LAURENCE
LUCILLE	LUCY	LUCIA
MARIE	MARIA	MIREILLE
MERRY	MERCY	MURRAY
PATTI	PATRIZIA	PATIENCE
ROSEMARY	SAGE	SAFFRON
SAMANTHA	SAMARA	SASKIA
SELMA	SELENA	SERENA
STACY	LACEY	MACY
STEPHANIE	STELLA	STORY
SHYANNE	CHEYENNE	WYOMING
TAMMY	TAMARA	TAMAR
WILMA	WILLOW	WILLA
ZENA	ZOE	ZORA

Boys

UNCOOL	COOL	COOLER
ADOLPH	ADRIAN	ADLAI
ALAN	ALCOTT	ALDO
ARNOLD	ARNE	ARNO
ARTHUR	ARCHER	ARTEMAS
ASHLEY	ASHER	ASH

UNCOOL	COOL	COOLER
BILL	WILL	LIAM
BRUCE	BRYCE	BRUNO
CHUCK	CHARLIE	CARLO
DARRYL	DARIUS	DASHIELL
DAVE	DAVIS	DAMON
DENNIS	DENNISON	DENVER
EDDIE	EDWARD	NED
HANK	HENRY	HARRY
IVAN	IVOR	IVO
JIMMY	JAMES	JAMESON
JOHN	JACK	GIACOMO
JEFF	JEB	JEX
KEN	BEN	XEN
KENNETH	KENYON	KENNEDY
LEON	LEO	LEONARDO
MANNY	EMANUEL	EMMETT
MILTON	MILES	MILO
MIKE	MAC	MAGUIRE
MONROE	JEFFERSON	TRUMAN
MONTY	MONTANA	MONTOYA
MORRIS	MORGAN	MORRISON
RAYMOND	RAY	RAOUL
RONALD	RONAN	ROONEY
THURSTON	THAYER	THADDEUS
WAYNE	KANE	ZANE
WILFRED	WILLIAM	WILLEM

Beatrix

British Names

et's face it, our baby-naming contemporaries across the Atlantic are often a step or two ahead of us. This means that some of the hottest names in Great Britain, Scotland, Ireland, and Wales, are still cool, underused choices over here. For instance:

Girls

AILSA	**AMELIA**
ALICE	**AMELIE**

ANABELLA	GRANIA
ANNABEL	
ANWEN	HERMIONE
AOIFE (pron. Eva)	HONORA
ARABELLA	
ARAMINTA	IMOGEN
BEATRIX	JEMIMA
BETHANY	
BRIONY/BRYONY	JESSAMINE
BRONWEN	JESSAMY
	JOCASTA
CATRIONA	
CHARLOTTE	KERENZA
CLEMENTINE	
CLOVER	LEATRICE
CRESSIDA	LETTICE
DAPHNE	MAEVE
	MAIREAD
ELSPETH	MAISIE
EUGENIE	MIA
	MILLIE
FIONA	MOIRA
FLORA	MYFANWY
GEMMA	NATALYA
GEORGINA	NATASHA

NICOLA

ORLA

PHILIPPA

PHOEBE

PIPPA

POPPY

RHIANNON

RHONWEN

SINEAD

SIOBHAN

SOPHIE

SORCHA

TAMSIN

UNA/OONA

UNITY

Boys

ADRIAN

ALISTAIR

AMBROSE

ANGUS

ARCHIE

ARRAN

AUGUSTINE

BALTHAZAR

BARNABY

BARNEY

BASIL

CALLUM/CALUM

CILLIAN

COLM

CONNOR

CORMAC

CRISPIN

DARAGH/
   DARRAGH

DECLAN

DUNCAN

EAMON

EUAN/EWAN

FELIX

FERGUS

FINLAY

COOLEST

HARRY POTTER NAME

• • •

Hermione

FRASER	NIALL
	NIGEL
GEORGE	NOEL
HAMISH	OWEN
HARRISON	
HARRY	PADRAIG
HUGH	PIERS
HUGO	
	QUENTIN
INIGO	
	REDMOND
JASPER	REECE/RHYS
	REYNOLD
KIAN	REX
KIERAN	ROBIN
KILLIAN	ROHAN/ROWAN
	ROLAND
LACHLAN	RONAN
LAIRD	RORY
LEWIS (#2 in	RUPERT
Scotland,	
#14 in England)/	SEAMUS
LOUIS	SEBASTIAN
LORCAN	
	TREVOR
MALACHY	TRISTAN
MALCOLM	

Tanguy

Foreign Names

F oreign names is another of those categories that is vast and almost uniformly cool, at least to the unschooled American ear (and we'd include our own in that category)—but beyond the reach of this book. For further selections, see our *Beyond Jennifer & Jason, Madison & Montana* as well as *Baby Names Now,* or search the Web for name sites overseas (try to find the real ones, not some American listing of Italian or French names—which often is incomplete and doesn't include the really interesting foreign choices). There are also a lot of foreign names sprinkled throughout this book. This group consists of those that didn't fit into any of

our other categories and that we think are especially appealing and, yes, cool.

Girls

ALEXANE	ELETTRA
ANIKA	ELIANA
ANJA	ELISKA
ANTHEA	ELODIE
ANTONELLA	ENORA
ARIELA	ESTELLA
AVELINA	
AZIZA	FEDERICA
	FERNANDA
BENICIA	FIA
BRIGITTE	FRANCESCA
	FYODORA
CALANDRA	
CALLA	GELSEY
CARMEN	GIANNA
CHANTAL	GIOIA
COSIMA	GRAZIANA
	GRAZIELLA
DANICA	GRETA
DELPHINE	GUADALUPE
ELEA	IMAN

INEZ	NADYA
INGRID	NATALYA
IRINA	NATASHA
IRINI	NIAMH (pron. Neev)
JANICA	PAOLA
JOZEFINA	PERDITA
	PETRA
KALILA	PIA
KALINDI	
KATYA	RAFFAELA/
	RAPHAELA
LAILA/LAYLA/	RENATA
LEILA	
LARISA	SANDRINE
LUDMILA	SANNE
LUDOVICA	SARITA
LUPE	SASKIA
	SAVITA
MALIA	SEVERINE
MANON	SIDRA
MANUELA	SIMONE
MARCELLA	SIRI
MARINA	SOLANGE
MARINE	SYBILLA
MARIT	SYLVIE/SILVIE
MIGNON	
	TATIANA

YELENA	FYODOR
ZUZANNA	GASTON
	GIANNI
	GRADY
Boys	GUIDO
	GUILLAUME
ALEXEI	GUSTAF
ANATOLI	
ANDREAS	HELIO
ANSELMO	
ARMANDO	ILYA
	IVAN
BAPTISTE	
	JANOS
CORENTIN	
CYR	KAZIMIR
	KRISTOF
DIMITRI	
	LAURENT
ELIAN	LEOPOLD
ELIO	LUC
ERASMO	LUCIEN
ETIENNE	
	MALO
FLANN	MAREK
FLYNN	MATEO
FRITZ	MIGUEL

MIKHAIL	TADDEO
MIKOLAS	TANGUY
	TIBOR
NICASIO	TOMASZ
NIKO	
	VASILI
PABLO	VLADIMIR
PAOLO	
PER	WOLF
PIER	
	UMBERTO
RAMON	
RAOUL	ZOLTAN
SERGEI	

Leon

What Europeans Call Cool

Ask young European parents what names they think are cool, and Americans are in for a real education. The ultimate lesson is that taste in names is culturally-specific and unpredictable. Consider these reports:

ITALY

Our friend and informal correspondent Claudio Aspesi reports that, among upper-middle-class Milanese parents, traditional and aristocratic names—some of them with an

Old German or Russian flavor—are coming back into style. These include:

Girls	Boys
ALLEGRA	FILIPPO
BEATRICE	FRANCESCO
BIANCA MARIA	GIOVANNI
CAROLINA	LORENZO
DESIDERIA	NICOLO
DOMITILLA	TANCREDI
FEDERICA	TOMMASO
FRANCESCA	
GIORGIA	
LUDOVICA	
MARIA	
MARTINA	

GERMANY

Here's an incredible fact to an American: The number one boy's name in Germany is (huge drumroll) none other than Leon. Yes, that Leon, a name that has become almost a joke in the U.S. but that in fact has a noble history as the Greek form (Leo is the Latin) for "lion." From Germany, Anja Toepper reports that classical names—as opposed to "American" choices—are coming back into favor. But there's a big difference between cool classical and old-fashioned names that, Toepper says, "would mean a punishment for a kid." If you want to find a German name for your child, avoid these traditional but highly uncool choices: for girls, Gerda, Gertrud, Hannelore, Hedwig, Elke, Ilse, and, for boys, Wilhelm, Heinz, Egon, Erwin, Franz, Jürgen, Hermann, Horst, Dietrich, Manfred, Gerhard, Kurt. The very fashionable classical names in Germany now are:

Girls	Boys
ANNA	BENJAMIN
HANNA	CLEMENS
JANA	FELIX
JOHANNA	JOHANNES
LENA	JONAS
LINA	LUCAS
LISA	VALENTIN

ENGLAND

The Brits always like traditional names, but they tend to be more game about reviving "old" choices than most Americans are. Clare Conville tells us from London that East Ender/Cockney names are back, and correspondent Ailsa

Gray, who lives in Wales, says that old-fashioned/Anglo-Saxon names sound new again. Some of the fashionable names in Britain include:

Girls	Boys
CECILY	ALBERT
CICELY	ALFRED
COCO	ARCHIE
DORA	ARTHUR
EDITH/EDIE	BARNEY
HERMIONE	BASIL
HONOR	FRANCIS/FRANK
IRIS	HARVEY
LETTICE	HUBERT
MAY	RAYMOND/RAY
MILLIE	STANLEY/STAN
MOLLY	
POPPY	

Sahara

Place Names

As a category, place names have been so well visited over the past decade that many selections from this group are no longer distinctive enough to be considered truly cool. However, some individual place names retain a fresh feeling and so still merit the official Seal of Coolness. For the most part, these are the more unusual choices as well as the more exotic places—or KINDS of places, which include rivers and national parks. However, a few old favorites—India stands out—are as cool as they ever were. Some place names can be used for boys but most now veer toward the feminine side.

ABILENE	CASPIAN
AFRICA	CATALINA
ALAMO	CAYMAN
ALBANY	CEYLON
ANDORRA	CHARLESTON
ANTARCTICA	CLUNY
AQUITAINE	COLOMBIA
ARABIA	CONNEMARA
ARAGON	CORSICA
ASPEN	CUBA
ASSISI	CYPRUS
ATLANTA	
ATLANTIS	DELPHI
AVALON	DENVER
	DOVER
BERLIN	DUBLIN
BIMINI	DUNE
BOLIVIA	
BOSTON	ELBA
BRASILIA	ENGLAND
BRAZIL	EVEREST
BRISTOL	
	GALWAY
CAIRO	GLASGOW
CALAIS	
CALEDONIA	HARLEM
CAMDEN	HAVANA
CARAGH	HOLLAND

HUDSON	PALERMO
	PANAMA
IBERIA	PERSIA
INDIA	PERU
INDRA/INDRE	PHILIPPINE
IRELAND	PORTLAND
JAMAICA	QUEBEC
JERSEY	QUINTANA
KENYA	RALEIGH
KINGSTON	RIO
KYOTO	ROMA
	ROMANY
LOUISIANA	
LOURDES	SAHARA
	SALEM
MEMPHIS	SAMARA
MIAMI	SAMOA
MILAN	SENEGAL
MOROCCO	SEVILLA
	SICILY
NAIROBI	SIENA
NILE	SONOMA
	SONORA
ODESSA	
OLYMPIA	TAHITI
	TANGIER

TIBET   VENICE

TRENTON   VIENNA

TRINIDAD

                 YORK

UMBRIA

                 ZION

VALENCIA

Jezebel & Jane

Bad Girl / Good Girl Names

It may be difficult for people on the brink of parenthood to acknowledge this, but it's cool to be bad. It was cool when you were younger . . . and it's still going to be cool when your baby-to-be is a lot lot older. And in this age of extremes, it's also cool to be good. Prime example: Madonna, whose own name makes both lists, gave her daughter the saintly name of Lourdes, the place where the Virgin Mary miraculously heals the sick, but calls her by the sultry nickname Lola. For further illustration of the bad girl/good girl concept and more name ideas for your own angelic hellion, consult the following list.

Bad Girls

	LANA
	LILITH
APHRODITE	LOLA
ASIA	LULU
BATHSHEBA	MABEL
BILLIE	MADONNA
	MAISIE
CAYENNE	MAMIE
CLEO	MITZI
COCO	MONIQUE
DELILAH	PANDORA
DESDEMONA	PEACHES
DIVA	PORTIA
DIXIE	
DOMINIQUE	QUEENIE
EGYPT	RAMONA
	RAVEN
FANNY	RIPLEY
FIFI	ROXANNE
FLAME	ROXIE/ROXY
	RUBY
GIGI	
	SADIE
JEZEBEL	SALOME

SCARLETT   BAY
SHEBA
STORM   CARA
                  CHARITY
TALLULAH   CHASTITY
TEMPEST   CLAIRE
TRIXIE   COMFORT
                  CONSTANCE

VENUS
                  DULCY
XENA
                  ELEANOR
YASMINE   ESTHER

ZULEIKA   FAITH
                  FELICITY
                  FLEUR
Good Girls   FLORA
                  FLOWER
ABIGAIL   FRANCES
ALICE   FREESIA
ALICIA
ALLEGRA   GRACE
ANEMONE
ANGELICA   HELEN
ANNA   HONOR
ARIEL   HOPE

JANE	POLLY
JULIA	POSEY
JUSTICE	PRIMROSE
	PRISCILLA
LAKE	PRUDENCE
LAURA	
LEAH	RACHEL
LILAC	ROSE
LILIA	RUTH
LOUISA	
LOURDES	SERAPHINA
	SERENA
MADONNA	SILENCE
MARGARET	SUNDAY
MARIA	
MARIAN	TEMPERANCE
MARTHA	TILLIE
MERCY	TRUE
MIMOSA	
MODESTY	UNITY
NORA	VERITY
	VIRGINIA
PANSY	
PATIENCE	WILLOW
PETUNIA	

Fred

Guy Names

There is a small but elite group of names that, while undoubtedly cool, are not unusual or different in any way. They're old-time, all-time guy names—think of them as the new Jack, Jake, Sam, and Max.

ART	CHET
	CY
BARNEY	
	FRANK
CAL	FRED
CHARLIE	

GEORGE   MOE

GIL

GUS   NAT

                NATE

HAL   NED

HANK   NICK

JOE   RALPH

LEW/LOU   WILL

MAC/MACK

Macauley

Mac Names

We've heard in the past few years of a lot of Macken-zies, McKennas, and McKaylas—in a wide array of spellings. Cute, maybe, but no longer are these three names cutting-edge cool. So, too, in recent years have other sur-name-names enjoyed widespread popularity, rendering such waspy favorites as Parker and Cooper beyond cool.

What's cool now is a combination of the two trends: Surname-names with the Mac (think Macaulay, as in Culkin) prefix. Of course, the coolest surnames are the ones you can lay genuine claim to from your family tree. But here's one idea: You can honor an ancestor by putting the

Mac prefix (which signifies 'son of') before his first name, so grandpa Arthur inspires baby Macarthur. Authentic or not, used for girls or boys, these choices are undeniably cool:

MACALLISTER	MCCARTHY
MACARDLE	MCCOY
MACARTHUR	MCDERMOTT
MACAULAY	MCELROY
MACKAY	MCENROE
MACLAREN	MCEWAN
MACLEAN	MCGRATH
MACMILLAN	MCKEON
MACREA	MCKINLEY
MAGEE	MCLAUGHLIN
MAGINNES	MCLEOD
MAGUIRE	MCMANUS
MCADAM	MCNALLY
MCAVOY	MCNEIL
MCCABE	MCPHERSON
MCCAREY	

Orlando

O Names

We said it in our very first baby-naming book, *Beyond Jennifer & Jason*, and we say it still: Names that begin or end with the letter 'o' are cool. Thankfully, the 'o' names remain unsullied, appealing choices all, especially (though there are a few feminine selections in this group) for boys. The options, of course, range far beyond those offered here, especially considering the entire world of Latinate names. This group just gives you a start.

ALAMO   ALONZO

ALDO   AMEDEO

ANTONIO	DINO
APOLLO	DJANGO
ARLO	DURANGO
ARMANDO	
ARNO	ECHO
	ELMO
BENECIO/	EMILIO
BENICIO	ENZO
BENNO	
BO	FERNANDO
BRUNO	FRISCO
CAIO	GIACOMO
CAIRO	GIORGIO
CALICO	
CALYPSO	HORATIO
CAMEO	HUGO
CARLO	
CATO	INDIGO
CICERO	INDIO
CLAUDIO	INIGO
CLEO	IVO
COLORADO	
CONSUELO	JERICHO
COSMO	JETHRO
DANILO	KYOTO
DIEGO	

LAREDO	OCTAVIO
LEANDRO	ODESSA
LEO	ODETTE
LEONARDO	ODILE
LIDO	ODIN
LORENZO	ODION
LUCIANO	OLAF
	OLGA
MARCO	OLIVER
MARINO	OLIVIA
MASSIMO	OLIVIER
MILO	OLWEN
MONTEGO	OLYMPIA
MOROCCO	OMAR
	OONA
NAVARRO	OPHELIA
NEMO	OREN
NICO	ORIANA
NICOLO	ORILIO
NILO	ORION
	ORLANDO
O'BRIEN	ORLY
O'HARA	ORSINO
O'KEEFE	ORSON
OAK	OSCAR
OBADIAH	OTIS
OBERON	OTTILIE
OCEAN	OTTO

OWEN	RODRIGO
OZ	ROLLO
OZIAS	
	SCORPIO
PABLO	SERGIO
PAOLO	SHILOH
PEDRO	STEFANO
PHILO	
PIERO	TADDEO
PLACIDO	THEO
PLATO	
PRIMO	VIGGO
PROVO	VITO
	VITTORIO
RENO	
REO	WALDO
RIO	
ROCCO	ZENO

COOLEST
PALINDROME NAME
• • •
Otto

Sophia

Bobo Cool Names

There is a certain kind of name that is considered cool by that segment of the upwardly mobile yet politically correct population so cleverly known as bobos—Bourgeois Bohemians, in the parlance of David Brooks's book *Bobos in Paradise.* Bobos like distinctive things but abhor ostentation; they have good taste but disdain convention; they appreciate the classics but like them with a modern twist. Most but not all of the names they favor are to the left of the most popular list, but far to the right of most choices in this book. You'll see them on the rosters of upscale nursery schools, hear them in the playgrounds of affluent neighborhoods, and you may like them yourself. And why not? They're good names, classic as well as cool, embodying style along with history. The only problem is that you may hear them far more than you want to in the years to come.

Girls

ABIGAIL	CLARA
ALEXA	CLAUDIA
ALICE	
ALLEGRA	DAISY
ANNA	DOROTHEA
ANNABEL	
AUDREY	ELEANOR
AVA	ELIZA
	ELLA
BEATRIX	EMMA
BELLA	EVA
	EVE
CAMILLA	
CARA	FELICITY
CARINA	FIONA
CAROLINA	FLORA
CECILY	FRANCES
CHARLOTTE	
CHLOE	GABRIELLA
CLAIRE	GEMMA

GEORGIA	MAISIE
GRACE	MARGARET
	MAUDE
HELEN	MAYA
HELENA	MIRANDA
HOPE	
	NATALIE
INDIA	NELL
ISABEL	NORA
ISABELLA	
IVY	OLIVIA
JACQUELINE	PIPER
JOSEPHINE	POLLY
JULIA	
JULIANA	ROSE
JULIET	
	SADIE
LAURA	SASHA
LEILA	SOPHIA
LILA	SOPHIE
LILY	STELLA
LOLA	SUSANNAH
LUCY	
	TESS
MABEL	
MADELEINE/	VIOLET
MADELINE	

WILLA   FELIX
                 FINN
ZOE   FORREST

                 GABRIEL
Boys   GEORGE
                 GRAHAM
AIDAN   GREGORY
ALEX   GUS
ANDREW
                 HARRISON
BARNABY   HARRY
                 HENRY
CALEB   HOMER
CALVIN
CHRISTIAN   ISAAC
CLAY   ISAIAH
COLE
COLIN   JACK
                 JACKSON
DASHIELL   JASPER
DOMINIC   JOE
DUNCAN   JONAH
                 JONAS
ELIJAH   JULIAN
EMMETT
ETHAN   LEO
EZRA   LIAM

LUCAS   QUINN

MALCOLM   REED
MILES

                 SEBASTIAN
NATHAN   SIMON
NATHANIEL   SPENCER
NED
NOAH   TOBIAS

OLIVER   WALKER
OSCAR   WYATT
OWEN

PATRICK

Q

Nicknames

Sometimes the whole nature of a name can be changed and cooled by using a fresh-sounding nickname, either as a short form or on its own. Many of the names that are heard today—such as Molly, Kate, Jack, and Toby—began as more informal versions of standard names. Here are some ideas for new-millennium nicknames, some of them revivals of old favorites, some of them foreign imports:

ASH	Asher, Ashley
BAS	Sebastian
BENNO	Benjamin
BETTA	Elizabeth
BIDU	Bridget
BRAM	Abraham
BREE	Briana
CALE	Caleb
CAM	Camilla
CARLO	Charles
CARO	Caroline
CASO	Cassandra
CAT	Catherine
CHAN	Chandler
CHARLIE	Charlotte
CHARTY	Charlotte
CHAY, CHAZ	Charles
CIA	Cynthia
CINDA	Cynthia, Lucinda
CLEM	Clementine
COZ	Cosmo
DAISY	Margaret
DASH	Dashiell
DEBO, DEBS	Deborah
DEX	Dexter

DEZ, DEZI	Desmond
DIX	Richard
DOE	Dorothea
DORO	Dorothea, Dorothy
DREA, DREE	Alexandria, Andrea
DREW	Andrew
DUNN	Duncan
FRANCE	Frances
FEE	Fiona
FLORY	Florence
FRITZI	Frederica
GEORGE	Georgia
GORE	Gordon
GRAM	Graham
GUS	Angus, August, Augusta
IBBY	Isabel
IMMY	Imogen
IZZY	Isaac, Isabel, Isadora
JAX	Jackson
JEM	Jemima, Jeremy
JULES	Julia, Julie
KAT	Katharine

COOLEST
ROYAL NAME
• • •

George

LAURO	Laurence
LETTY	Elizabeth
LIAM	William
LIV, LIVIA, LIVY	Olivia
LOLA	Dolores, Lolita, Lourdes, Paloma
LOLO	Caroline
LULU	Louise
MABBS	Mabel
MAGO	Margaret
MAISIE	Margaret
MAMIE	Mary
MANO	Emanuel
MASO	Thomas
MELIA	Amelia
MITZI	Mary, Miriam
MO	Maureen
NED	Edward
NELL, NELLY	Eleanor, Ellen, Helen
NESSA	Vanessa
NICO	Nicholas
O	Olivia, Otis, Owen
OZ, OZZIE	Oscar
PATIA	Patricia
PIP	Phillip

PIPPA	Philippa
POLLY	Mary, Pauline
POM	Thomas
PRU	Prudence
Q	Quentin, Quincy
RAFE	Ralph, Raphael
SACHA, SASHA	Alexander, Alexandra
SADIE	Sarah
SEB	Sebastian
SIMM, SIMS	Simeon, Simon
SKY	Schuyler, Skyler
SUKEY	Susannah
TADDEO	Theodore
TANSY	Anastasia
TESS, TESSA	Teresa
TIBBIE	Elizabeth
TONIO	Anthony
TRIXIE	Beatrix
TRU	Truman
VAN	Vanessa
WILL	Willa
WILLS	William

XAN, ZAN	Alexander
Z	Zachary et al.
ZANDER	Alexander

II. COOL COOL

...

Famous Names

Heath

Celebrity Names

A cool name seems as essential an ingredient of stardom today as a well-sculpted body and a killer smile, a fact that can hardly be lost on parents in search of a name that will help launch their child in the world. Some of these names—Jada is a notable example—are inspiring thousands of namesakes, but their real power as a group is in making parents feel that, when it comes to names, special means beautiful, talented, and famous. While names of current stars are most influential, some favorites from the past—Audrey and Ava, for instance—are also proving inspirational.

AIDAN Quinn

AISHA Taylor

ANANDA Lewis

ANASTACIA

ANGELINA Jolie

ANJELICA Huston

ANOUK Aimée

ASHTON Kutcher

AVRIL Lavigne

BAI Ling

BALTHAZAR Getty

BENICIO Del Toro

BEYONCÉ Knowles

BJORK

BLU Cantrell

BRECKIN Meyer

CALISTA Flockhart

CAMERON Diaz

CAMRYN Manheim

CATE Blanchett

CHAKA Khan

CHARLIZE Theron

CHINA Chow

CHLOE Sevigny

CLEA DuVall

CRISPIN Glover

CUBA Gooding, Jr.

Matt DAMON/
    DAMON Wayans

DELROY Lindo

DEMI Moore

DENZEL Washington

DERMOT Mulroney

DIVA Zappa

DJIMON Hounsou

DONOVAN Leitch

DOUGRAY Scott

DREA DeMatteo

DREW Barrymore

ELLE MacPherson

EMO Phillips

ENRIQUE Iglesias

ENYA

ESAI Morales

EWAN McGregor

FAIRUZA Balk

FAMKE Jannsen

FRANKA Potente

GARCELLE Beauvais-Nilon

GISELE Bündchen

GLENN Close (female)

GRIFFIN Dunne

GWYNETH Paltrow

HALLE Berry

HARRISON Ford

HAYDEN Christenson

HEATH Ledger

IBEN Hjejle

ILEANA Douglas

IONE Skye

Keenen IVORY Wayans

JACINDA Barrett

JADA Pinkett Smith

JAMES King (female)

JAVIER Bardem

JENA Malone

JOAQUIN Phoenix

JOLIE, Angelina

JUDE Law

JUDGE Reinhold

JULIETTE Binoche

KEANU Reeves

KEENEN Ivory Wayans

KIEFER Sutherland

KYRA Sedgwick

LAKE Bell

LEELEE Sobieski

LEONARDO DiCaprio

LIAM Neeson

LIEV Schreiber

LIV Tyler

Jennifer LOVE Hewitt

MARISKA Hargitay

MARLEY Shelton

MENA Suvari

MILLA Jovovich

MINNIE Driver

MONET Mazur

MOON Unit Zappa

NEVE Campbell

NICOLLETTE Sheridan

OLIVIER Martinez

OMAR Epps

ORLANDO Jones

OWEN Wilson

PARKER Posey

PERI Gilpin

PIERCE Brosnan

PINK

PORTIA de Rossi

POSEY, Parker

RALPH (pron. Rafe) Fiennes

REESE Witherspoon

ROSARIO Dawson

SADE

SAFFRON Burrows

SALMA Hayek

SAVION Glover

SCARLETT Johansson

SELA Ward

SIGOURNEY Weaver

SKEET Ulrich

SOFIA Coppola

SOLEDAD O'Brien

STELLAN Skarsgård

STOCKARD Channing

SUMMER Phoenix

TALISA Soto

TAYE Diggs

TÉA Leoni

THANDIE Newton

THORA Birch

TILDA Swinton

TOBEY Maguire

TRAYLOR Howard

TYRA Banks

UMA Thurman

VIGGO Mortensen

VIN Diesel

VING Rhames

VIVICA Fox

WINONA Ryder

ZOOEY Deschanel

Petal

Movie Character Names

The only names cooler than stars' names right now are the names of the characters they play. In fact, with the exception of Jack, which seems to be the name of the male lead in every other movie these days, characters' names veer from the unusual to the outlandish. A few, such as Trinity from *The Matrix*, are moving up the popularity charts. Others may prove inspirational to you. Here, a sam-

COOLEST
SOUTHERN BELLE NAME
• • •
Delilah

pling of cool character names along with the stars who play
them and the films in which they appear.

AKASHA	Aaliyah	*Queen of the Damned*
AMELIE	Audrey Tautou	*Amelie*
AMSTERDAM	Leonardo DiCaprio	*Gangs of New York*
ARWEN	Liv Tyler	*The Lord of the Rings Trilogy*
AZRAEL	Jason Lee	*Dogma*
BARTLEBY	Ben Affleck	*Dogma*
	Christian Glover	*Bartleby*
BJERGEN	Drew Barrymore	*Wayne's World 2*
BONANZA	Rain Phoenix	*Even Cowgirls Get the Blues*
BULLSEYE	Colin Farrell	*Daredevil*
CASH	Don Cheadle	*The Family Man*
CASTOR	John Travolta/ Nicolas Cage	*Face/Off*
CHAKA	Chris Rock	*Jay & Silent Bob Strike Back*
CHASE	Nicole Kidman	*Batman Forever*
CHESNEY	Joey Lauren Adams	*Harvard Man*
CHILI	John Travolta	*Get Shorty*
CHRISTANEL	Jennifer Ehle	*Possession*
CISCO	Mark Addy	*Down to Earth*
CLERICK	Christian Bale	*Equilibrium*
CLOVE	Jennifer Aniston	*The Thin Pink Line*
CODY	Elisabeth Shue	*Bad Girls*

COTTON	Liev Schreiber	*Scream 2*
CYRUS	Selma Blair	*Down to You*
DEMILLE	Robert Sean Leonard	*Driven*
DESI	Julia Stiles	*O*
DEVLIN	George Clooney	*Spy Kids*
DOVA	Matt Dillon	*Albino Alligator*
DOYLE	Samuel L. Jackson	*Changing Lanes*
DRAVEN	Cuba Gooding, Jr.	*In the Shadows*
ELEKTRA	Jennifer Garner	*Daredevil*
ELLE	Reese Witherspoon	*Legally Blonde*
ELMO	Samuel L. Jackson	*Formula 51*
EMIRA	Lela Rochon	*Why Do Fools Fall in Love*
ETHNE	Kate Hudson	*Four Feathers*
EVANNA	Jessica Capshaw	*Minority Report*
FAUNIA	Nicole Kidman	*The Human Stain*
FRIDA	Salma Hayek	*Frida*
GREEN	Shalom Harlow	*How to Lose a Guy in Ten Days*
HANSEL	Owen Wilson	*Zoolander*
IMOGEN	Julia Stiles	*Down to You*
JERZY	George Clooney	*Welcome to Collinwood*
JJACKS *(sic)*	Keanu Reeves	*Feeling Minnesota*
JINX	Halle Berry	*Die Another Day*
JUBA	Djimon Hounsou	*Gladiator*
KAENA	Kirsten Dunst	*Kaena: The Prophecy*
KORBEN	Bruce Willis	*The Fifth Element*

LIDDA	Kirsten Dunst	*Luckytown Blues*
LOKI	Matt Damon	*Dogma*
LONGFELLOW	Adam Sandler	*Mr. Deeds*
LUX	Kirsten Dunst	*Virgin Suicides*
MACE	Samuel L. Jackson	*Star Wars: Episode II—Attack of the Clones*
MAXIMUS	Russell Crowe	*Gladiator*
MIRTHA	Penelope Cruz	*Blow*
MORPHEUS	Laurence Fishburne	*The Matrix*
NEO	Keanu Reeves	*The Matrix*
NOVALEE	Natalie Portman	*Where the Heart Is*
OBERON	Heath Ledger	*Paws*
ORORO	Halle Berry	*X-Men*
PADMÉ AMIDALA	Natalie Portman	*Star Wars: Episode II—Attack of the Clones*
PARIS	Marisa Tomei	*Dirk and Betty*
PELAGIA	Penelope Cruz	*Captain Corelli's Mandolin*
PETAL	Cate Blanchett	*The Shipping News*
PETUNIA	Fima Shaw	*Harry Potter Series*
PISTACHIO	Dana Carvey	*The Master of Disguise*
PLUTO	Eddie Murphy	*Pluto Nash*
POLEXIA	Anna Paquin	*Almost Famous*
RHEYA	Natascha McElhone	*Solaris*
ROUX	Johnny Depp	*Chocolat*

SALA	Catherine Zeta Jones	*The Phantom*
SATINE	Nicole Kidman	*Moulin Rouge*
SCHMALLY	Rachael Leigh Cook	*Scorched*
SERENDIPITY	Salma Hayek	*Dogma*
SERLEENA	Lara Flynn Boyle	*Men in Black 2*
SHARONNA	Heather Graham	*The Guru*
STEENA	Debi Mazar	*The Tuxedo*
SULLIVAN	Richard Gere	*Dr. T and the Women*
TERRA	Rain Phoenix	*Facade*
TORRANCE	Kirsten Dunst	*Bring It On*
TOULA	Nia Vardalos	*My Big Fat Greek Wedding*
TRINITY	Carrie-Anne Moss	*The Matrix*
TRIP	Josh Hartnett	*The Virgin Suicides*
ULYSSES	George Clooney	*O Brother, Where Art Thou?*
VIVI	Ashley Judd	*Divine Secrets of the Ya-Ya Sisterhood*
WOO	Jada Pinkett Smith	*Woo*
WREN	Elijah Wood	*Black and White*
ZINAIDA	Kirsten Dunst	*All Forgotten*

Klonoa

Video Game Names

Movie character names may seem both inspired and inspirational to parents in the first decade of the twenty-first century, but what of the next generation of parents-to-be, those raised not on movies and television but on video games? Their idea of a cool name is sure to be way wilder than that of parents today. These names from current popular video games will give you an idea of the kind of choices that might inspire the names of your grandchildren.

Girls	Boys
AOI	AIDYN
	AKUJI
KAIRI	ALUCARD
	ARC
LARA	ASH
MARIE	BANJO
PAI	CLOUD
	CRASH
QUISTIS	
	DANTE
RINOA	DAXTER
	DUKE
SAMUS	
SELPHIE	GOEMON
SHION	
	ICO
TAKI	
	JAK
YUNA	JOJO
ZELDA	KAGE
	KAIN

KAZOOIE   SPYRO
KLONOA   SQUALL

LINK   TIDUS
                 TOAN
MAJORA
MAXIMO   VYSE
MUNCH
                 YOSHI
PARAPPA
                 ZELL
RAIDEN   ZIDAN
RYGAR
RYU

Rafferty

Celebrity Baby Names

Baby-naming seems to be a competitive sport in Hollywood. The goal: To come up with the coolest name in town—a difficult task when your colleague's babies are named Rafferty (Jude Law and Sadie Frost), Bechet (Woody Allen's daughter), and True (along with Sonnet and Ocean, the children of Forest Whitaker).

And what are we poor mortals to do, hearing such baby names? If not follow suit by naming our own children Rafferty and Bechet, then at least feeling inspired to be a bit more adventurous in our own choices of names. Just as celebrities influence our taste in clothes and hair and makeup, so, too, do they give us a new model for baby-naming.

Here, the coolest celebrity baby names of recent years, the famous parents who chose them, along with our thinking on why the names belong in this category.

AIDAN ROSE   *Faith Daniels*
This was the first time we heard this Irish boy's name given to a girl, and we think it made a graceful gender switch.

ALAIA   *Stephen Baldwin*
Not only unusual, but also extremely haunting and lyrical. It's the last name of French designer Azzedine.

ALCHAMY   *Lance Hendriksen*
This *Millennium* cast member took a word with magical associations, modified its spelling, and bestowed it on his daughter.

AMAI ZACHARY   *Marlon Wayans*
At first glance this name may seem to be merely a new and improved twist on Amy/Aimee, but it also carries a deeper meaning. In the Japanese culture, Amai means the sense a well-loved child has of being cherished by her parents—a worthy name, and feeling, to pass on to your own beloved. Zachary, the last name of little Amai's mother, makes a fine first name for a girl.

AMANDINE *John Malkovich*
A unique Gallic name with a French sense of style. Plus, it has an appealingly nutty flavor.

AMELIA GRAY *Lisa Rinna & Harry Hamlin*
A long-neglected Victorian name that's a cooler, more distinctive choice than the similar-in-feel but more ordinary Amanda or Emily, and the middle name adds to its muted charm.

ANAIS *Noel Gallagher*
The guiding force of Oasis undoubtedly took as his naming inspiration the famed novelist and diarist, Anaïs Nin.

ATTICUS *Isabella Hoffman & Daniel Baldwin*
A name so weighty it becomes almost whimsical, associated by most people with the noble lawyer played by Gregory Peck in the classic *To Kill a Mockingbird*.

AUGUST *Garth Brooks*
The man in the black hat almost single-handedly made this male name unisex when he used it for his daughter. A much cooler choice than either the too-flimsy Summer or the too-serious Augusta, or the dated April and June.

AVA *Aidan Quinn / Heather Locklear & Richie Sambora / Reese Witherspoon & Ryan Philippe / Gil Bellows*

Obviously, a hot current celebrity favorite, Ava radiates the sultry retro glamour of Ava Gardner.

BECHET DUMAINE   *Woody Allen*
The clarinet-playing Allen chose to honor one of his musical heroes, Sidney Bechet, when he gave this name to his daughter.

BELLA   *Keenen Ivory Wayans / Eddie Murphy*
Bella—along with Isabella and Ella and Gabriella—is among the premiere cool names for girls in Hollywood.

BLUE ANGEL   *Dave Evans*
U2's "The Edge" earns his own epithet in making this fringe choice for his daughter.

CALEDONIA   *Shawn Colvin*
The old poetic name for Scotland becomes a fresh-sounding place name for a girl.

CHESTER   *Rita Wilson & Tom Hanks*
It's not fusty, it's fashionable, purely because this megawatt Hollywood couple chose it.

CICELY   *Sandra Bernhard*
The hard-edged comic made a surprisingly frilly choice for her daughter with this Victorian-valentine name.

CLARA   *Ewan McGregor*

Just as Americans are rediscovering Claire, leave it to a Brit to home in on its quainter-sounding variation.

COCO (Short for COLETTE)
Dylan McDermott & Shiva Rose/Sting

If it hadn't been for Chanel, Coco would have remained only a monkey's name. In this case, it's a cute and creative short form of COLETTE, a multiasseted name: it has French éclat plus a strong literary association.

DASHIELL   *Cate Blanchett/Harry Anderson/Lisa Rinna & Harry Hamlin/Alice Cooper*

A lot of dash and a touch of mystery thanks to detective writer Dashiell Hammett.

DELANEY   *Martina McBride*

A hot, but still cool, Irish surname that had possible musical associations for this country singer.

DELILAH   *Lisa Rinna & Harry Hamlin*

The quintessential seductive name. How can a Delilah not be gorgeous, and cool?

DENIM KOLE   *Toni Braxton*

Named after Denham, a character in *To Sir with Love*. But substituting K's for C's is no longer kool.

DEX *Dana Carvey*
Every name with an x in it is cool. Yes, even Xavier.

DEXTER *Diane Keaton*
A nerdy boy's name comes alive when given to a girl.

EJA *Shania Twain*
This unusual phonetic spelling of Asia gives the name a more masculine flavor.

ELLA *Kelly Preston & John Travolta/Annette Bening & Warren Beatty/Gary Sinise*
When Emily reached number one and became too widely used, and Emma became the standard-issue yuppie baby name, Ella ascended to its current position as a premiere cool name. Plus how can you miss with the Ella Fitzgerald connection?

ELLERY *Laura Dern*
If Ella is cool for a girl then it stands to reason that Ellery, a name associated with old-time mystery writer Ellery Queen (the pen name for a two-cousin team), would be equally cool for a boy. Similarly, the George Stephanapolises brought Elliott into the girls' camp.

ESMÉ *Tracy Pollan & Michael J. Fox/Samantha Morton/ Anthony Edwards*
A captivating J. D. Salinger–inspired choice.

ESTHER ROSE   *Ewan McGregor*

A perfect companion name for sister Clara, Esther is one of those so-clunky-it's-almost-cool names. A star's child, rich and famous, has a head start on pulling off a name like this.

EULALIA   *Marcia Gay Harden*

Southern, soft, sweet, and far out of the ordinary.

FINNIGAN   *Eric McCormack*

A perfect blend of first and last name, the combination embodies an irrepressible Irish energy.

GIACOMO   *Sting*

An appealing example of an ethnic import that can combine seamlessly with a short Anglo surname.

GIDEON   *Mandy Patinkin*

A strong but underused Biblical name.

GULLIVER   *Gary Oldman*

Perhaps only the actor who would play Sid Vicious might choose a name this outré, but it does have an engaging energy.

HOLDEN   *Dennis Miller/Rick Schroder*

Another Salinger-character-inspired name.

HOMER   *Bill Murray/Richard Gere & Carey Lowell/Anne Heche*

Yes, Homer, one of the old-fangled names sidling back into

favor, often used to honor an ancestor, as in the case of Richard Gere's father.

HOPE   *Brad Garrett*
The most optimistic of names.

INDIO   *Deborah Falconer & Robert Downey, Jr.*
We know of several female Indias, but this boy may be the unique Indio, which can be thought of as a California desert place name.

IRELAND   *Kim Basinger & Alec Baldwin*
An interesting girl's name that moves beyond the boundaries of the usual geographical territories.

IRIS   *Sadie Frost & Jude Law*
Floral names like Rose and Lily are spreading like wildflowers, but this cool British couple dared to pick a bloom that has been long out of fashion and so make it sound new again.

ITALIA   *LL Cool J*
A winner because it retains its native form.

JASPER   *Don Johnson*
A British-style choice that has both backbone and style, a combination difficult to find in a boy's name, with an artistic association to painter Jasper Johns.

JUDAH MIRO   *Lucy Lawless*

A neglected Old Testament name with the appealing short form, Jude. Like Jasper, Miro has interesting painterly connections.

KAI   *Jennifer Connelly*

Kai is on the beach, with a tan and a surfboard. What's cooler than that?

KAIA JORDAN   *Cindy Crawford*

This choice is more straightforward and at the same time hipper than overused kousins Kayla, Kylie, et al.

LENNON   *Patsy Kensit & Liam Gallagher*

Naming a child after your hero gives him two degrees of cool: a name with real meaning and a positive image to reach toward.

LOLA   *Annie Lennox/Kelly Ripa/Chris Rock*

Madonna's use of Lola as the nickname for her daughter Lourdes brought this name from the smoky back room to center stage in terms of style.

LOURDES   *Madonna*

An unexpectedly spiritual choice for the Material Girl, with its religious/place associations.

LULU   *Edie Brickell & Paul Simon*
Spunky and saucy, Lulu straddles the line between campy and cool.

MABEL   *Tracey Ullman*
Ditto.

MASON   *Kelsey Grammar*
Fine for a boy, cooler for Frasier Crane's little girl.

MEMPHIS   *Bono*
One of the more original and alluring of the place name names, especially effective when combined with a feminine middle name like Eve (as Bono did).

MERCEDES   *Val Kilmer & Joanne Whalley*
An elegant Spanish name with obviously luxe connotations that makes a smooth transatlantic passage.

MILO   *Ricki Lake/Camryn Manheim*
Jaunty.

OCEAN   *Forest Whitaker*
Retro charm—Hippie days are here again (the other Whitaker children are named True and Sonnet).

PALOMA   *Emilio Estevez*
Foreign style combined with a lovely sound and appealing meaning—dove, symbol of peace.

PIPER   *Gillian Anderson / Brian De Palma / Melissa Sue Anderson*
High energy and music.

POPPY HONEY   *"Naked" Chef Jamie Oliver*
Poppy is cool, Honey a little gooey, when combined they
sound more like recipe ingredients than a name.

RAFFERTY   *Sadie Frost & Jude Law*
One of the coolest of the Irish surnames, with a raffish quality all its own.

RAYMOND   *Rebecca Broussard & Jack Nicholson*
Using the short form Ray, as in Charles, is an easy way to be
cool when naming a boy or a girl. Nicholson and Broussard
went hard-core hip in reviving this relic.

ROAN   *Sharon Stone*
A strong, red-haired Irish name.

ROAN GREEN   *Uma Thurman & Ethan Hawke*
Green is Hawke's middle name, and fits in perfectly with the
new palette of color names becoming so stylish.

ROCCO   *Madonna*
The power of Madonna: making this muscle-bound he-man
name cool outside of Sicily.

ROMEO *Victoria "Posh Spice" and David Beckham*
Until very recently, this was in the so-far-out-it-will-always-be-out category, but in today's more liberal baby-naming climate, that classification has all but disappeared; and Romeo can be seen as a valid Shakespearean choice.

RUBY *Matthew Modine/Suzanne Vega/Rod Stewart*
See LOLA and MABEL.

SADIE *Joan Allen/Michael Ontkean/Elvira*
See LOLA, MABEL, and RUBY.

SALOME VIOLETTA *Alex Kingston*
The ultimate Biblical bad-girl name (it actually means "peace"), Salome is another newly viable choice, and Violetta is an enchanting Irish import.

SATCHEL *Spike Lee/Woody Allen*
This was an extremely cool choice when Woody Allen revived it from baseball history—Satchel Paige was a great early black ballplayer—and gave it to his son. The only way to follow such a baby-naming act was when director Spike Lee used the name for his daughter.

COOLEST

GLAMOUR GIRL NAME

• • •

Ava

SEVEN *Erykah Badu*
On *Seinfeld*, George once decided that the ultimate cool baby name

was a number, Seven. Singer and actress Badu apparently agreed.

TAJ *Steven Tyler*
Short, catchy, and exotically imaginative.

TALLULAH *Demi Moore / Bruce Willis*
This pair launched the cool starbaby name concept when they chose SCOUT and RUMER as well as the more user-friendly Tallulah for their girls.

TRUMAN *Rita Wilson & Tom Hanks*
Seriously, almost presidentially, cool.

WALLIS *Anthony Edwards*
Rescued from single-owner purgatory (via the Duchess of Windsor) and given new life.

WILLOW *Will Smith and Jada Pinkett Smith*
A graceful nature name that also relates to Dad's name (as son Jaden's does to Mom's).

XEN *Tisha Campbell-Martin*
Given that "X" is pronounced as "Z," this name has a serene, spiritual aura.

ZOLA *Eddie Murphy*
As seductive as Lola, but with a distinctive twist.

SUPER (MODEL) COOL

Along with long legs and gorgeous smiles, many supermod-
els also seem to have a talent for picking cool names for their
kids. Some examples:

ALEXANDRIA ZAHRA	Iman
AUDEN	Amber Valletta
AURELIUS CY	Elle Macpherson
CAIRO	Beverly Peele
CASPAR	Claudia Schiffer
CECILY	Stella Tennant
ELIZABETH SCARLETT	Jerry Hall
FRANKIE-JEAN	Donna D'Errico
GABRIEL LUKE BEAUREGARD	Jerry Hall
GEORGIA MAY AYEESHA	Jerry Hall
HANNA FELICIA	Vendela
HARRY	Stephanie Seymour
IZABELLA	Hunter Tylo
JAMES LEROY AUGUSTINE	Jerry Hall

JULIA ANNETTE	Vendela
LILA GRACE	Kate Moss
MARCEL	Stella Tennant
MINGUS	Helena Christensen
PRESLEY	Cindy Crawford
SAILOR	Christie Brinkley
YANNICK FAUSTO	Daniela Pestova

Monet

Artist Names

Artists (and architects and designers) are almost by definition cool, and their names are part of the package. Parents can capture some of that creative spirit by choosing one of these artist names for their baby, and at the same time give their child an inspirational role model. The following list encompasses both first (JASPER Johns) and last (CALDER) names, which have been drawn from all over the aesthetic map, from fine art to fashion.

AALTO	AMEDEO
ALAIA	ANSEL

AZZEDINE	EAMES
	EERO
BLAKE	ELLIS
BOHAN	
BRAQUE	FORD
	FRIDA
CALDER	
CARO	GABO
CELLINI	GAUGUIN
CHANEL	GEHRY
CHARDIN	GEORGIA
CHIRICO	GERRIT
CHRISTO	GOYA
CLAES	GRECO
COCO	
COLE	HARDY
CONRAN	HARTIGAN
CORNELL	HOMER
COROT	HOPPER
CRISTOBAL	
CURRIER	INDIANA
CY	INIGO
	ISSEY
DELAUNAY	IVES
DIX	
DONATELLO	JACKSON
DUFY	JASPER
	JUDD

KAHLO	MORISOT
KAMALI	
KENZO	O'KEEFFE
KLEE	
KRIZIA	PABLO
	PALOMA
LAUTREC	PEI
LEGER	PELLI
LEONARDO	PIANO
	PICABIA
MAGRITTE	PICASSO
MAILLOL	PIET
MANET	PONTI
MANOLO	
MANZU	QUANT
MARIN	
MARISOL	RABANNE
MATTA	RAEBURN
MIES	RAPHAEL
MILLAIS	REM
MILLET	REMINGTON
MIRO	ROBBIA
MIUCCIA	RODIN
MONET	ROUSSEAU
MOORE	RYDER
MORANDI	
MOREAU	SARGENT
MORI	SERRA

SHAHN   VIEIRA
SIMONETTA   VIGEE
SOUTINE   VIONNET
SULLY

                 WESTON
TAMAYO   WILLEM
TITIAN   WINSLOW
TOULOUSE
TURNER   YVES

VALENTINA   ZANDRA
VALENTINO

Thelonious

Musician Names

Since musicians invented the concept of cool, where better to look for naming inspiration than to their own names?

AALIYAH	ARETHA
ABBA	ARLO
ADEMA	ARMSTRONG
AJA	ASHANTI
ALANIS	AUDRA
ALANNAH	AVRIL
AMADEUS	AXL

BASIA	DINAH
BAEZ	DION
BECHET	DIXIE
BECK	DJANGO (pron. Jango)
BENATAR	DONOVAN
BESSIE	DUFF
BEYONCÉ	DURAN
BILLIE	DYLAN
BING	
BIX	EARTHA
BJORK	ELLA
BONO	ELLINGTON
BOWIE	ELTON
BRAHMS	ELVIS
	ENO
CAB	ENRIQUE
CALE	ENYA
CALLAS	ETTA
CALLOWAY	EVERLY
CARUSO	
CHAKA	FABRIZIO
COLE	
COLTRANE	GARCIA
CROSBY	GARTH
	GENESIS
DENVER	GERSHWIN
DEVO	GILLESPIE
DEXTER	GUTHRIE

HARRISON   MEHTA

HENDRIX   MILES

                  MINGUS

IGGY   MORRISEY

ISAAC   MORRISON

                  MOS

JABBO   MOZART

JACKSON   MULLIGAN

JAGGER

JAHEIM   NASH

JOPLIN   NAT

                  NELLY

KAI   NICA

KITT

                  ODETTA

LATIFAH   OTIS

LENNON   OZZY

LENNOX

LIONEL   PIAF

LOUIS   PINK

LUCIANO   PRESLEY

MACY   QUINCY

MADONNA

MAHALIA   RAMONE

MARIAH   RAVI

MARLEY   RAY

MCCARTNEY   RUFUS

SADE   VILLELLA (dance)

SANTANA

SHANIA   WOLFGANG

SINEAD   WYNTON

SULLIVAN

                        ZEVON

TALIB   ZUBIN

THELONIUS

VEGA

VERDI

Ludacris

Rap Names

Names of rappers take the universe of possibilities into a whole other galaxy, one that few parents, at least right now, will want to visit. Not to be too academic about this, but rap names have their basis in the double-naming tradition that dates back to the very beginnings of African-American culture, when slaves used the names imposed by their masters when white folk were around, and other names—African names, day names, nicknames—when they were with friends and family. So while it might be ludicrous at this point to think of naming your child after rapper Ludacris, the boundary-breaking nature of rap names promises to inspire more adventurous choices—even if just for their kids' nicknames—among hip-hop-loving parents in the future. Here, a few of the rap names around today:

BIZZY	LIL BOW WOW,
BUSTA RHYMES	LIL KIM,
	LIL ZANE
DJ SHADOW	LUDACRIS
DMX	
DR DRE	MACE
	MOS DEF
EAZY E1	MYSTIKAL
50 CENT	QUEEN LATIFAH
ICE CUBE	SISQO
ICE T	SNOOP DOGG
JA RULE	TALIB KWELI
JAY-Z	

Dashiell

Literary Names

Literary inspiration can arise from both the names of authors and the characters they create. Here are some suggestions coming from the first and last names of writers ranging from Edgar Allen Poe to Zadie Smith, and characters from the pages of books spanning various periods of literary history. But in this category, as always, feel free to think about your own personal favorites:

AUTHORS

ALCOTT

AMIS

ANAÏS

ANGELOU

APHRA

AUDEN

AUGUST

AUSTEN

AYN

BALDWIN

BALLARD

BECKETT

BEHAN

BELLOW

BENET

BLAKE

BLY

BRONTË

BYATT

BYRON

CAIN

CARSON

CARVER

CHANDLER

CHEEVER

CONRAD

COOPER

CRANE

DANTE

DASHIELL

DIDION

DJUNA

DYLAN

ELIOT

ELLISON

EMERSON

EUDORA

FITZGERALD

FLANNERY

FORSTER

FROST

GALWAY

GIDE

GLASGOW

COOLEST

IRISH PLACE NAME

• • •

Donegal

HADLEY	MALLARMÉ
HAMMETT	MAYA
HARPER	MCEWAN
HART	MEHTA
HARTE	MILAN
HEMINGWAY	MILLAY
HUGO	MORRISON
	MOSS
ISHMAEL	MUNRO
JARRELL	NERUDA
JERZY	NIN
JESSAMYN	NORRIS
JULES	
	O'CASEY
KEATS	
KEROUAC	PAZ
KESEY	PLATO
	PO
LAFCADIO	POE
LALITA	
LANGSTON	RALEIGH
LARDNER	RHYS
LECARRÉ	RING
LONDON	ROALD
LOWELL	ROTH
	RUMER

SALINGER	TWAIN
SAROYAN	
SHAW	VIDAL

TENNESSEE	WALKER
TENNYSON	WILLA
THACKERAY	YEATS
THEROUX	
THISBE	ZADIE
THOREAU	ZANE
THURBER	ZOLA
TRUMAN	ZORA

CHARACTERS

FEMALE

ALABAMA	*Save Me the Waltz*	Zelda Fitzgerald
AMARYLLIS	*Back to Methuselah*	George Bernard Shaw
AMORET	*The Faerie Queen*	Edmund Spenser
ANTONIA	*My Ántonia*	Willa Cather
ARABELLA	*The Pickwick Papers*	Charles Dickens
ARIADNE	*Heartbreak House*	George Bernard Shaw
AURORA	*Terms of Endearment*	Larry McMurtry

BATHSHEBA	*Far From the Madding Crowd*	Thomas Hardy
BRETT	*The Sun Also Rises*	Ernest Hemingway
BRIANA	*The Faerie Queen*	Edmund Spenser
BRIONY	*Atonement*	Ian McEwan
CANDIDA	*Candida*	George Bernard Shaw
CATALINA	*The High Road*	Edna O'Brien
CATRIONA	*Catriona*	Robert Louis Stevenson
CHARITY	*Martin Chuzzlewitt*	Charles Dickens
CHARMIAN	*Antony and Cleopatra*	William Shakespeare
CLARICE	*The Silence of the Lambs*	Thomas Harris
CLARISSA	*Mrs. Dalloway*	Virginia Woolf
CLEA	*Alexandria Quartet*	Lawrence Durrell
CRESSIDA	*Troilus and Cressida*	William Shakespeare
CYANE	*Metamorphoses*	Ovid
DAHLIA	*Carry On, Jeeves*	P. G. Wodehouse
DAISY	*The Great Gatsby*	F. Scott Fitzgerald
DENVER	*Beloved*	Toni Morrison
DESDEMONA	*Othello*	William Shakespeare
DOMENICA	*Unconditional Surrender*	Evelyn Waugh
EMMA	*Emma*	Jane Austen
ESMÉ	*For Esmé—With Love and Squalor*	J. D. Salinger

EVANGELINE	*Evangeline*	Henry Wadsworth Longfellow
FAUNIA	*The Human Stain*	Philip Roth
FEATHER	*Bad Boy Brawly Brown*	Walter Mosley
FLEUR	*The Forsyte Saga*	John Galsworthy
GINEVRA	*Villette*	Charlotte Brontë
GUINEVERE	*Le Morte D'Arthur*	Sir Thomas Malory
HANA	*The English Patient*	Michael Ondaatje
HAYDÉE	*The Count of Monte Cristo*	Alexandre Dumas
HONORA	*Sea Glass*	Anita Shreve
HONORIA	*Bleak House*	Charles Dickens
	and *Babylon Revisited*	F. Scott Fitzgerald
HYACINTH	*The Princess Casamassima*	Henry James
ISADORA	*Fear of Flying*	Erica Jong
ISOLDE	*Tristan and Isolde*	
JACY	*The Last Picture Show*	Larry McMurtry
JADINE	*Tar Baby*	Toni Morrison
JULIET	*Romeo and Juliet*	William Shakespeare
JUNO	*Juno and the Paycock*	Sean O'Casey
KINSEY	*A is for Alibi,* etc.	Sue Grafton
LOLITA	*Lolita*	Vladimir Nabokov
MAISIE	*What Maisie Knew*	Henry James
MALTA	*Bleak House*	Charles Dickens
MAMIE	*The Ambassadors*	Henry James

MARIGOLD	*Quartet in Autumn*	Barbara Pym
MARIN	*A Book of Common Prayer*	Joan Didion
MELANCTHA	*Three Lives*	Gertrude Stein
NARCISSA	*Sartoris*	William Faulkner
NENNA	*Offshore*	Penelope Fitzgerald
NERISSA	*The Merchant of Venice*	William Shakespeare
NINETTA	*Nicholas Nickleby*	Charles Dickens
NIOBE	*Metamorphoses*	Ovid
NOKOMIS	*Hiawatha*	Henry Wadsworth Longfellow
ORLEANNA	*The Poisonwood Bible*	Barbara Kingsolver
PANSY	*The Portrait of a Lady*	Henry James
PECOLA	*The Bluest Eye*	Toni Morrison
PEYTON	*Lie Down in Darkness*	William Styron
PILAR	*For Whom the Bell Tolls*	Ernest Hemingway
PLEASANT	*Our Mutual Friend*	Charles Dickens
PORTIA	*The Merchant of Venice*	William Shakespeare
PRAIRIE	*Vineland*	Thomas Pynchon
RAIN	*The Sandcastle*	Iris Murdoch
RIMA	*Green Mansions*	William H. Hudson
ROMOLA	*Romola*	George Eliot
ROSAMOND	*Middlemarch*	George Eliot
SABRA	*Cimarron*	Edna Ferber
SCARLETT	*Gone With the Wind*	Margaret Mitchell

SCOUT	*To Kill a Mockingbird*	Harper Lee
SETHE	*Beloved*	Toni Morrison
SIDDA/ SIDDALEE	*Divine Secrets of the Ya-Ya Sisterhood*	Rebecca Wells
STELLA	*A Streetcar Named Desire*	Tennessee Williams
SULA	*Sula*	Toni Morrison
TAMORA	*Titus Andronicus*	William Shakespeare
TAMSIN	*A Few Green Leaves*	Barbara Pym
TEMPLE	*Sanctuary*	William Faulkner
UNDINE	*The Custom of the Country*	Edith Wharton
VELVET	*National Velvet*	Enid Bagnold
VERENA	*The Bostonians*	Henry James
VIDA	*Vida*	Marge Piercy
VIVI	*Divine Secrets of the Ya-Ya Sisterhood*	Rebecca Wells
VIVIETTE	*Two on a Tower*	Thomas Hardy
ZULEIKA	*Zuleika Dobson*	Max Beerbohm

MALE

AMORY	*This Side of Paradise*	F. Scott Fitzgerald
ARCHER	*The Age of Innocence*	Edith Wharton
ATTICUS	*To Kill a Mockingbird*	Harper Lee
AURIC	*Goldfinger*	Ian Fleming
AXEL	*Victory*	Joseph Conrad
BARLEY	*The Russia House*	John Le Carré

BARNABY	*Barnaby Rudge*	Charles Dickens
BEALE	*What Maisie Knew*	Henry James
BENVOLIO	*Romeo and Juliet*	William Shakespeare
BRICK	*Cat on a Hot Tin Roof*	Tennessee Williams
BROM	*The Legend of Sleepy Hollow*	Washington Irving
CASPAR	*Portrait of a Lady*	Henry James
CATO	*Henry and Cato*	Iris Murdoch
CHANCE	*Being There*	Jerzy Kosinski
CLEMENT	*Return of the Native*	Thomas Hardy
CLEON	*Pericles*	William Shakespeare
CODY	*Visions of Cody*	Jack Kerouac
CORIN	*As You Like It*	William Shakespeare
DARCY (surname)	*Pride and Prejudice*	Jane Austen
DARL	*As I Lay Dying*	William Faulkner
DORIAN	*The Picture of Dorian Gray*	Oscar Wilde
FENNO	*Three Junes*	Julia Glass
FITZWILLIAM	*Pride and Prejudice*	Jane Austen
GUITAR	*Song of Solomon*	Toni Morrison
GULLIVER	*Gulliver's Travels*	Jonathan Swift
HEATHCLIFF	*Wuthering Heights*	Emily Brontë
HIERONYMOUS/ HARRY	*City of Bones*	Michael Connelly
HOLDEN	*The Catcher in the Rye*	J. D. Salinger
ISHMAEL	*Moby Dick*	Herman Melville
JAPHY	*Dharma Bums*	Jack Kerouac

JARVIS	*A Tale of Two Cities*	Charles Dickens
JASPER	*The Pathfinder*	James Fenimore Cooper
JOLYON	*The Forsyte Saga*	John Galsworthy
JUDE	*Jude the Obscure*	Thomas Hardy
LAIRD	*In the Gloaming*	Alice Elliot Dark
LEMUEL	*Gulliver's Travels*	Jonathan Swift
LOCH	*The Golden Apples*	Eudora Welty
MACON	*Song of Solomon*	Toni Morrison
	and *The Accidental Tourist*	Anne Tyler
MARIUS	*Les Misérables*	Victor Hugo
MELCHIOR	*Brideshead Revisited*	Evelyn Waugh
MILO	*Catch-22*	Joseph Heller
MOR	*The Sandcastle*	Iris Murdoch
NEWLAND	*The Age of Innocence*	Edith Wharton
ORLANDO	*Orlando*	Virginia Woolf
PRAXIS	*Praxis*	Fay Weldon
QUEBEC	*Bleak House*	Charles Dickens
QUILLEN	*Sea Glass*	Anita Shreve
QUINTAS	*Titus Andronicus*	William Shakespeare
RHETT	*Gone With the Wind*	Margaret Mitchell
RILEY	*The Grass Harp*	Truman Capote
ROARK (surname)	*The Fountainhead*	Ayn Rand
RODION	*Crime and Punishment*	Fyodor Dostoevsky
ROMEO	*Romeo and Juliet*	William Shakespeare
RUFUS	*A Death in the Family*	James Agee

SANTIAGO	*The Old Man and the Sea*	Ernest Hemingway
SAWYER (surname)	*The Adventures of Tom Sawyer*	Mark Twain
SEBASTIAN	*Brideshead Revisited*	Evelyn Waugh
SENECA	*Babbitt*	Sinclair Lewis
SEPTIMUS	*The Mystery of Edwin Drood*	Charles Dickens
SHANE	*Shane*	Jack Warner Schaefer
SILAS	*Silas Marner*	George Eliot
TAFT	*End Zone*	Don DeLillo
TRISTAN	*Tristan and Isolde*	
TRISTRAM	*Tristram Shandy*	Laurence Sterne
UTAH	*Under Milkwood*	D. M. Thomas
VIVALDO	*Another Country*	James Baldwin
WOLF	*The Sea Wolf*	Jack London
YANCEY	*Cimarron*	Edna Ferber
ZOOEY	*Franny and Zooey*	J. D. Salinger

And don't forget two of the coolest of all:

FABLE

STORY

Grayer

Nanny Diary Names

The heroine of the smash novel *The Nanny Diaries* may be named simply Nanny, but her young charges and their friends have a fantastic collection of names. The choices are a perfect meeting of the realistic and the ridiculous:

Girls

ALEX   **BENSON**
ALLISON

CRISTABELLE

ELLIE

GISELLE

JOSEPHINA

LULU

STANTON

Boys

ADDISON
ALEX

CARSON
CARTER
CHRISTIANSON

DARWIN

GRAYER

TINFORD

Venus

Athlete Names

Most of the legendary stars of sports history have regular guy names like Joe and Jimmy and Michael and Mickey (not to mention Billie Jean), but some of the newer stars—as well as the surnames of the classics—offer options that go beyond the perimeters of that limited playing field:

ALI	BO
ASHE	BORIS
	BRANCH
BECKER	BROOKS
BJORN	

CAL	ISIAH
CAREW	IVAN
CLEMENTE	
COE	JACKSON
CORBETT	JORDAN
	JOSS
DANIRA	
DEION	KAREEM
DEMPSEY	KENYON
	KNUTE
EARLY	KOBE
EMBRY	
EMMETT	LANDRY
EVANDER	LENNOX
EWING	LUTE
	LUTHER
FISK	
FRAZIER	MAGIC
	MALONE
GABRIELLA	MARINO
GARVEY	MARIS
GEHRIG	MARQUIS
GRIFFEY	MARTINA
	MCENROE
HANK	MIA
HOGAN	MONTANA
HUNTER	

NOLAN	TIGER
	TIKI
PALMER	TINKER
PAYTON	TRIS
PELE	TROY
PICABO	TUNNEY
REESE	VENTURA
RONDE	VENUS
	VIJAY
SABO	
SARAZEN	WEST
SERENA	
SHAQUILLE	ZELMO
THROPE	
THURMAN	

COOLEST
WINTERBABY NAME
• • •
Frost

III. PRE-COOL COOL

. . .

Old Names

Aurelia

Ancient Names

*O*ver the centuries, throughout the Western cultures, there have been thousands upon thousands of names lost to fashion. Okay, we can live without Baldric and Ethelbert, but many other ancient names—from Rome and Byzantium, from old England and Germany—deserve to be unearthed in the interest of cool. Here's a selection of worthy ancient names, from a range of eras and places, that have possibilities in the modern world.

Girls

CYRA

ABELIA	DAMARIS
AMICA	DAMIANE
ANNIA	DECIMA
APHRA	DELICIA
APPHIAH	DENNOT
AQUILIA	DOMINICA
ARRECINA	DRUSILLA
ARRIA	
ATARAH	ELIZABELLA
ATHALIA	ELLOT
AURELIA	EPHRAM
AVITIA	
	FABIA
BASILIA	FANNIA
BEATA	FERELITH
	FLAVIA
CALVINA	
CAMPANA	GALLA
CANDIDA	GAYNOR
CESARIA	GWENORE
CHAUNCEY	
CLEMENCIA	HILARIA
COLUMBA	HONORIA
CRISLI	
CRISPINA	ISOLDE

JENNET	PASSARA
JOLECIA	PATERIA
JONET	PERPETUA
JUNO	PERSIS
JUSTINA	PETRONEL
	PHILLIDA
LAURENCIA	PLACIDIA
LIVIA	PRIMULA
MAHALA	RAYNE
MARABLE	
MARCIANA	SABINA
MELISENT	SINETTA
MERAUDE	
MERIALL	TACE
MINERVA	TANAQUIL
MIREILLE (pron.	TITIANA
Meer–ay)	TROTH
MUCIA	TULLIA
	TURIA
NICASIA	
	VERINA
OCTAVIA	VISTILIA
	VIVIANA
PACCIA	
PALATINA	ZELINA
PARNELL	

COOLEST
COUNTRY MUSIC NAME
• • •
Twain

Boys

	MENAS
AENEAS	NAZARES
ALBAN	
ANDREAS	PRIMUS
APOLLOS	
ATTICUS	REMUS
AUGUSTUS	ROMANUS
AURELIUS	ROMULUS
CASSIUS	SEPTIMUS
CATO	SEVERUS
CLAUDIUS	STEPHANUS
COSMAS	
CYRUS	TACITUS
	TARQUIN
DEMETRIUS	THEON
	THURSTAN
LAZARUS	TIBERIUS
LOVELL	TITUS
LYELL	
	URBAN
MAGNUS	
MARCELLUS	ZEBEDEE
MAURUS	ZENO
MAXIMUS	

Moses

Holy Names

S ome of the coolest names we've come across in researching this book were found in the least likely of sources: the Bible and guides to the saints. If you want to know the provenance of the names that follow—who Lydia was in the Bible, for instance, or what made St. Swithun so special—you're going to have to consult a source that deals with that sort of hard information. We're just here to tell you that these names are cool . . . and won't make the priest blanch at the baptismal font.

Girls

HADASSAH

ADAH

JAEL

ANASTASIA

JEMIMA

ANNICE

JERUSHA

APOLLONIA

AQUILINA

KETURAH

AZUBAH

KEZIAH

LILITH

BARBARA

LUCY

BERNADETTE

LYDIA

BETHIA

BIBIANA

MARA

MICHAL

CEARA

MORGANA

CECILY

MORIAH

DARIA

NATALIE

DEBORAH

DELILAH

PRISCILLA

DELPHINA

DINAH

RIONA

RUTH

EVE

SANCHIA

FABIOLA

SAPPHIRA

FAITH

SARAI

TABITHA	BRUNO
TALITHA	
TAMAR	CALEB
TATIANA	CASSIAN
THEA	CLEMENT
	CLETE
ZILLAH	CONALL
	CONAN
	CRISPIN

Boys

	CYPRIAN
	CYRIAC
ABEL	
ABNER	DECLAN
ABRAHAM	DONATE
ADLAI	DUNSTAN
ALBAN	
AMBROSE	EPHRAIM
ANSELM	ERASMUS
AUBREY	ESAU
	EZEKIEL
BARZILLAI	EZRA
BASIL	
BECAN	FABIAN
BENET	FELIX
BENNO	FINNIAN
BLASE	
BOAZ	GABRIEL
BROGAN	GERMAIN

> COOLEST
> SPICE NAME
> • • •
> *Saffron*

GERVASE	MALACHI
GIDEON	MATTHIAS
GILES	MICAH
	MOSES
ISAAC	
ISAIAH	NOE
JABEZ	OMAR
JADON	OSWIN
JAPHETH	
JAVAN	PIRAN
JETHRO	
JOAB	QUENTIN
JOACHIM	
JUBAL	RAPHAEL
JUDAH	REMI
JULIAN	REUBEN
	ROMAN
KENELM	RUPERT
KILIAN	
	SAMSON
LAMBERT	SAUL
LAZARUS	SEBASTIAN
LEMUEL	SIMEON
LEVI	SIMON
LINUS	SIXTUS
LUCIAN	SWITHUN

TIARNAN	WOLFRAN
TITUS	WOLSTON
TOBIAH	
	ZACHARIAS
URBAN	ZEBEDIAH
	ZEDEKIAH
VITAL	

BIBLICAL PLACE NAMES

ABILENE	JERICHO
ADAMAH	
AZEKAN	KEILAH
BETHANY	PELLA
BOZRAH	PETRI
CALAH	SAMARIA
CARMEL	SELA
	SHEBA
EDEN	SHILOH
GAZA	TAMAR
IVAH	ZION

Amias

Colonial Names

Many of the names that were widely used in the U.S. during colonial times have fallen out of favor for long enough now that many sound fresh and even cool again. If you like historic names but want to move beyond the Victorian and biblical choices we've heard so much of in recent years, consider these names culled from Revolutionary War rolls and eighteenth-century town histories. The only caveat: The choices are much wider and more appealing for boys than for girls.

Girls

ABITHA

APPHIA

BELLE

CORNELIA

DORCAS

ELIZA

EMELINE

ESTER

FANNY

HENRIETTA

LYDIA

PHILA

PHOEBE

PRUDENCE

ROSANNA

SELAH

SUSANNA

THEODOSIA

Boys

ABIEL

ABIJAH

ABIMAEL

ABRAM

ABSALOM

ADONIJAH

ALDEN

AMIAS/AMYAS

AMIEL

AMMIRAS

AMOS

AMZI

ARCHIBALD

ASA

ASAHEL

ASHER

AZARIAH

BALTHASAR	HIRAM
BARNABAS	HOMER
BARTHOLOMEW	HORATIO
BAZEL	
BENAJAH	ISHAM
	ISRAEL
COMFORT	
CONSTANT	JARED
CYRUS	JEDIDIAH
	JEHU
EBENEZER	JEREMIAH
ELEAZAR	JONAS
ELI	JOSIAH
ELIAB	JOTHAN
ELIAS	
ELIHU	LAZARUS
ELIJAH	LEMUEL
ELIPHALET	LEVI
ELISHA	LINUS
EMANUEL	
EMORY	MICAJAH
ENOCH	
	OBADIAH
GARRETT	OBED
HALMACH	PHILOMON
HANNIBAL	PHINEAS
HEZEKIAH	

REASON   URI

RUFUS

                   ZACHARIAH

SAMSON   ZADOCK

SETH   ZEBULON

SOLOMON   ZIBA

THADDEUS

THANKFUL

Murray

Grandpa / Granddaughter Names

Blame it on Sidney. This name with thick glasses, a snowfall of dandruff on its shoulders, and plaid polyester pants pulled up to its sternum sounds nothing less than charming, nothing less than cool when applied to a little girl. And so too can the other Old Man names here. Caution: **Do not attempt to bestow any of these names on a boy.** The world is not yet ready for another generation of male Seymours and Stanleys.

ALLEN   BARRY

ARTHUR

CECIL	PERRY
CYRIL	
	RANDOLPH
GARY	ROY
HOWARD	SEYMOUR
	SHELDON
IRA	SHERMAN
	SIDNEY
JAY	STANLEY
	STUART
LAWRENCE	
LYLE	THEODORE
MARSHALL	VAUGHN
MAURY	VERNON
MORLEY	VINCENT
MURRAY	
	WALLACE
NEIL	WAYNE
NORRIS	

COOLEST
VICTORIAN NAME
• • •
Jasper

Agnes

Old Lady Cool

If you like that fusty old feel but you're not ready to go all the way to Murray for your daughter, you might want to consider the elderly lady names here, cool by virtue of their very disdain for fashion.

ADA	AUGUSTA
ADELIA	
AGATHA	BEATRICE
AGNES	BLANCHE
ANASTASIA	
ANTONIA	CLARA

CLAUDIA	KAY
CORA	
CORDELIA	LAVINIA
CORNELIA	LEONORA
	LETITIA
DORA	LOUISE
DOROTHEA	
	MATILDA
EDITH	MAY
ELLA	MURIEL
ESTHER	MYRTLE
EUGENIA	
	OLIVE
FAY	
FLORA	PEARL
FLORENCE	
FRANCES	ROSALIND
	RUTH
HARRIET	
HAZEL	SYLVIA
HELEN	
HENRIETTA	THEODORA
IVY	VIOLA
	VIOLET
JOSEPHINE	
JUNE	WINIFRED

Norbert

Names No One May Be
Cool Enough For

You have to be pretty damn cool to name your kid Norbert, cool in that "I like it and I don't care what the world thinks" kind of way. Except you're not the one who's going to have to deal with having the name Norbert when you play Little League. You're not the one who's going to have to introduce yourself as Norbert to girls in bars. In fact, if you think it's so cool, maybe you should change your own name to Norbert and not saddle a poor little kid with it.

The point: While we can appreciate the cool inherent

in these clunky names, we fear that few human beings are cool enough to actually have one of them.

Girls

IRMA

BERTHA

JOYCE

BEULAH

MILDRED

DORIS

MYRNA

EDNA

PHYLLIS

ELSIE

ETHEL

SHIRLEY

EUNICE

WANDA

FRIEDA

GAY

Boys

GERTRUDE

GRISELDA

ARNOLD

HELGA

BERNARD

HEPZIBAH

BERTRAM

HESTER

BURTON

HILDEGARDE

HORTENSE

DELBERT

EDGAR   NORBERT

ELMER

EUGENE   OSBERT

                 OSWALD

FRANKLIN

                 SEYMOUR

HARVEY   SHELDON

HERMAN   SHERMAN

HUBERT   SIGFRIED

HYMAN

                 VERNON

IRVING

                 WILBUR

JULIUS   WILFRED

MAURICE

MELVIN

MERVYN

MILTON

IV. NEW COOL

...

Creative Names

Zaiden

Invented Names

For many prospective parents, the definition of a cool name is one that is unique. People are looking for names that will make their children stand out and apart from the crowd, and seek to achieve this either through creating a new spelling for an established name, or inventing a completely new name.

This taste for one-of-a-kind names is not surprising when you consider that many new moms and dads grew up with megapopular names themselves and felt that it sacrificed some of their individuality. For instance, from 1970 to

1985, for a period of fifteen years, Jennifer was the number one name across the country. Masses of women now of childbearing age were one of four or five Jennifers in their class, and the name became so generic that there are now Jennifer support groups on the Internet and a Society for the Prevention of Parents Naming Their Children Jennifer. There were almost equal numbers of Jessicas, Amandas, Lisas, Michelles, Amys, and Heathers, not to mention all those Jeffs, Joshes, Jonathans, and Jasons.

In a larger sense, there is a general feeling of depersonalization and lack of distinctive identity in this era of ID codes and pin numbers, causing many parents to want to create a singular appellation for their children. And then there's the movement over the past decade or so toward increasingly unusual names, with new ethnic names, place names, surname-names, and words-as-names jumping into the mix. The parent who wants a truly distinctive name for her baby has to move further than ever away from the established roster of names.

For parents who want to create a unique name, here are some techniques:

1. Take a name whose sound appeals to you—this seems to work better for boys' names—change the first initial and play with the spelling if you like to make it rhyme. (We've also seen this trend happen with conventional names, with a somewhat more unusual choice—Mason—replacing its near-identical twin Jason.)

AIDAN=CAIDEN/KADEN, TAIDEN, ZAIDEN,
    BRAIDEN/BRAYDEN, JADEN/JAYDON
ALLAN=CALLAN/KALLAN, DALLIN
AMOS=RAMOS, TAMOS
ANTON=CANTON, DANTON, JANTON, ZANTON
ARLO=DARLO, VARLO, ZARLO
BAILEY=ZAILEY
BARNEY=CARNEY/KARNEY, VARNEY, ZARNEY
CHRISTIAN=TRISTIAN
COLTON=BOLTON, DOLTON
DALTON=BALTON, CALTON, GALTON, RALTON
DARREN-JARREN/JARON, GARON, ZARREN
DERRICK=TERRICK, JERRICK, ZERRICK
DEVIN/KEVIN=BREVIN, JEVIN, TEVIN/TEVON
DYLAN=KYLAN, RYLAN
ETHAN=KETHAN, LETHAN
GABE=CABE, LABE, TABE, ZABE
GAVIN=DAVIN, KAVIN, TRAVON
HAYDEN=BRAYDEN/BRADEN, CAYDEN/CADEN/KAYDEN/
    KADEN, GRADEN, JAYDEN, SHADEN, TADEN, ZADEN/
    ZAYDEN
JACKSON=BRAXON, DAXON, MAXON, PAXON
JASON=BRASON, CASON, TAYSON
KEVIN=NEVAN, TEVIN
KIERNAN=TIERNAN
LEO=KEO, REO, TEO, ZEO
LOGAN=BROGAN, ROGAN
PIERCE=KIERCE

RILEY=BRILEY
TYLER=KYLER, SYLER, ZYLER
TYSON=BRYSON, DYSON, KYSON
WADE=CADE, DADE, ZADE
ZANE=THANE

2. Or you can approach it from the other direction and add another letter/syllable at the end:

ASH=ASHTON
BLAKE=BLAKEN
BRENT=BRENTON
BRYCE=BRYSON/BRYCEN
CADE=CADEN/CAYDEN/KADIN/KAIDEN/KADEN
CASE=CASON
CHASE=CHASEN
GREY=GREYSON, GREYER
JAY=JAYDEN, JAYLAN
KEITH=KEITHEN
KIRK=KIRKER
KYLE=KYLER/KYLAN
TRENT=TRENTON
TREY=TREYNOR, TREYTON

3. Another technique, this one as old as ElizaBETH and EuGENE, is to drop the first syllable or syllables, or even an initial letter of a name. These days, for instance, Drew and

Ward are cooler than Andy or Ed. Here are some other possibilities, but as with most recipes, feel free to improvise.

(H)	ARLEY
(Pris)	CILLA
(Mal)	COLM
(An)	DREA
(An)	JELICA
(Eze)	KIEL
(O)	LIVIA
(A)	LONZO
(A)	MANDA
(A)	MELIA
(Ca)	MILLA
(Ara)	MINTA
(Cor)	NELIA
(Va)	NESSA
(Vero)	NICA
(Law)	RENCE
(Ad)	RIAN
(Je)	REMY
(Gab)	RIELLA
(Ana)	STASIA
(Mon)	TANA
(Oc)	TAVIA
(Ma)	TILDA
(Syl)	VIA
(Ir)	VING

COOLEST
FLOWER NAME
• • •
Violet

(Ale) **XANDER**

(Ale) **XANDRA**

(A) **ZIZA**

NAME.DOT.COM

Accents and hyphens have been around for a long time, used mainly to indicate pronunciation or link a double name: think Renee-Therese. Then accents and hyphens started straying to places they didn't technically belong, all in the service of making names more interesting, more unusual, cooler (Singer/actress Brandy called her daughter Sy'rai). Now the new way to add punctuation interest to a name is with the—what else?—dot, as in the ubiquitous dot.com. Singer India.arie is perhaps the best-known example of this, but hip-hoppers Will.i.am and apl.d.apl of the Black Eyed Peas have joined in, transforming the practice from a one-person aberration to a trend.

Vrai

Foreign-word Names

Two of the coolest trends right now are word names and foreign names, so why not combine the two? We combed our own *diccionarios* for French, Italian, and Spanish words that could make perfectly appropriate, attractive names for your baby, but no reason to stop here. Consider words from the language of your own ethnic background, be it Czech or Chinese, and add them to the list of your personal possibilities.

FRENCH

AERIEN	airy
ALEA	chance
ALIZÉ	soft cloud
ALOUETTE	lark
AMANDE	almond
AMBRETTE	almond seed
AMÉRIQUE	America
ANGE	angel
ANNEAU	ring, ringlet
ATLANTIQUE	Atlantic
BECHETTE	little spade
BICHETTE	little doe
BIJOU	jewel
BLEU	blue
BONTÉ	goodness, bounty
BRIN	sprig
CADEAU	gift
CANDIDE	open, frank
CHATON	kitten
DÉJÀ	already
DELÀ	beyond
DÉLICE	delight

DIMANCHE	Sunday
DORÉ	gilded
ELLE	she
FABRIQUE	fabric
FLAMBEAU	flame, candle
FLEUR	flower
FLEURETTE	little flower
FRAISE	strawberry
GALETTE	flat cake
IÇI	here
JADIS	in olden times
JAMAIS	never
JANVIER	January
JETON	marker, token
JOLIE	pretty
JUMELLE	twin
LARIGOT	ancient flute
LEXIQUE	lexicon, vocabulary
LIVRET	little book
LORIOT	oriole
LUMIÈRE	light
LUNE	moon

MAI	May
MAISON	house
MARDI	Tuesday
MARÉE	tide
MARGAY	tiger cat
MARRON	chestnut
MAUVE	seagull
MELILOT	sweet clover
MERISE	wild cherry
MIRABELLE	yellow plum
MOINEAU	sparrow
MUSIQUE	music
NEIGE	snow
NÉVÉ	compacted snow
NICHÉE	nest of young birds
PARC	park
PLAIRE	to please
POMME	apple
PREUX	gallant
REINE	queen
RIVAGE	shore
ROCHE	rock
ROUX	reddish brown
RUBAN	ribbon

SABINE	juniper tree
SAFRAN	saffron
SAISON	season
SAMEDI	Saturday
SANSONNET	starling
SATINÉ	satiny
SAVARIN	round cake
SÉJOUR	sojourn
SEMAINE	week
SOLEIL	sun
SOMMET	summit
SONGE	dream
TERRE	earth
TULIPE	tulip
VELOUTÉ	velvety
VICTOIRE	victory
VRAI	true
VRILLE	tendril
ZINGARO	gypsy

ITALIAN

ADAGIO	slowly, gently
AIO	tutor, teacher

ALBA	dawn
ALEA	chance, risk
ALITO	breath, light breeze
ALLEGRO	cheerful, merry
ALMA	soul
ALZATA	rising up, elevation
ANNATA	year's time
AQUILA	eagle
ARDESIA	slate
ARIA	air
AURETTA	gentle breeze
AURORA	dawn
BACCA	berry
BAIA	bay
BALIA	power, authority, also children's nurse
BALZO	leap
BELLEZZA	beauty
BENNATO	wellborn, generous
BIANCO	white
BLU	blue
BRIO	spirit, animation
CADENZA	cadence
CALA	cove, bay
CALIA	gold dust
CALLAIA	passage
CANNA	cane, reed

CAREZZA	caress
CIELO	sky
COLOMBA	dove
CORO	chorus
DANZA	dance, ball
DELFINO	dolphin
DESINATA	feast
DONNINA	good woman, clever girl
DOVIZIA	wealth, abundance
DUNA	dune
ELÈTTA	choice, elite
ÈLLERA	ivy
ELLISE	ellipse
FABBRO	inventor
FARÒ	lighthouse
FÈ	faith
FIAMMA	flame
FIERO	proud
FIORE	flower
FRANGIA	fringe
GÈLSO	mulberry
GEMELLA	twin sister
GÈMMA	jewel
GIADA	jade

GIOVANETTA	young girl
GRAZIA	grace
LAURO	laurel tree
LAVANDA	lavender
LILLA	lilac
LILLIALE	lilylike, white as a lily
LINDEZZA	neatness
LUNA	moon
MAGGIO	May
MANO	hand
MARÈNA	Morello cherry
MARRONE	maroon, chestnut
MASSIMO	maximum, supreme
MATITA	pencil
MATTOLINA	woodlark
MIRA	aim
MIRANDO	wonderful
MORGANA	mirage
NERO	black
NEVATA	snowfall
NEVE	snow
OLANDA	Holland
OMBRA	shadow

ONDA	wave
ORA	hour
PASQUA	Easter
PATRIA	native land
PÈRLA	pearl
PRIMA	first
RIVA	seashore
RIVO	stream, brook
ROANO	roan horse
SABBIA	sand
SALITA	ascent
SCALA	stairs
SERENELLA	lilac
STELLINA	little star
TAMIA	small squirrel
TERRA	earth
TRINA	lace
VALENTIA	skill, cleverness, bravery
VALLETTA	little valley
VENTURA	destiny, fate
VERO	truth
VIA	way, street

VIOLETTA	violet
VITA	life
ZANA	basket, cradle

SPANISH

ALA	wing
ALBA	dawn
ALEGRIA	gaiety
ALETA	wing
ALONDRA	lark
ALZA	rise
AMAPOLA	Poppy
ARO	ring, hoop
AURORA	dawn
AVELLANA	hazel tree
BAHIA	bay
BAYA	berry
BLANCA	white
BRIO	energy
CADENA	chain
CALA	cove
CANELA	cinnamon
CARICIA	caress

CEDRO	cedar
CHARRA	horsewoman
CIELO	sky
COLINA	hill
CONCHA	shell
CORTESIA	courtesy
CRUZ	cross
DIA	day
ESTRELLA	star
FLOR	flower
GALÁN	romantic hero
GALAXIA	galaxy
GANA	wish, desire
GARBO	poise
GAVIOTA	seagull
INDIO	Indian
ISLA	island
JABÓN	soap
JACA	pony
JACINTO	hyacinth
JAZMIN	jasmine
JOYA	jewel
JUBILO	joy

LAGO	lake
LEAL	loyal
LIENZO	linen
LOA	praise
LONA	canvas
LUNA	moon
LUZ	light
MAJO	nice
MAÑA	skill
MAREA	tide
MATIZ	shade, nuance
MEJILLA	cheek
MIRA	sight
OLA	wave
ORILLA	shore
PALOMA	pigeon, dove
PERLA	pearl
QUINTA	villa
REINA	queen
RENO	reindeer
RUBI	ruby

SABIO	wise
SEMILLA	seed

TALLA	carving
TIA	aunt
TIERRA	country
TIZA	chalk
TRAZA	appearance

VAJILLA	dishes
VALETA	weather vane
VEGA	fertile plain
VELADA	evening
VENTURA	happiness, luck
VIDA	life

ZAFIRO	sapphire

Pax

Spiritual Names

The post–September 11 world is more attuned to spirituality than ever. These names that suggest qualities we'd all like our children to aspire to fit our new definition of cool. While they seem as if they can work for both genders, most have been veering toward the feminine side. A few, such as Trinity, Destiny, Sky, and Genesis, had already been moving up the girls' popularity lists; many of the others might be fresh suggestions for either a boy or a girl, or for a middle name if too extreme for a first.

ANGEL	INFINITY
ANSWER	
ARCADIA	JUSTICE
BLISS	KISMET
CALM	LIGHT
CHANCE	
	MIRACLE
DESTINY	MYSTERY
DIVINITY	
DREAM	PAX
	PEACE
EDEN	PROMISE
ETHEREAL	
EVER	REMEMBER
EXPERIENCE	
	SECRET
FORTUNE	SERENDIPITY
	SERENITY
GENESIS	SKY
GUARDIAN	SPIRIT
GUIDE	
	TAROT
HALCYON	TRINITY
HARMONY	TRUE
HEAVEN	TRUST

Indigo

Color Names

Amber started it, and then Rose drove the point home. Now color names have exploded beyond these once-cool favorites to include hues from the obvious—Gray and Teal—to the most exotic, from Azure to Zinc. Recently Blue has taken off, primarily as a middle name: Cher was one of the first to use it for her son Elijah, and now we have Jackson Blue (Maria Bello), John Travolta and Kelly Preston's gallicized Ella Bleu, and the rocker Dave (U2) Evan's daughter Blue Angel. A new entry was seen when superstar couple Uma Thurman and Ethan Hawke chose Roan Green for their son. The full spectrum:

ALIZARIN	FUCHSIA
AMETHYST	
ANILINE	GRANITE
AQUA	GRAY/GREY
ASH	GREEN
AUBURN	GREIGE
AZURE	
	HAZEL
BEIGE	HENNA
BRICK	HYACINTH
BROWN	
BUFF	INDIGO
BURGUNDY	IVORY
CERISE	
CERULEAN	JADE
CHAMOIS (pron.	LAVENDER
shammy)	
CITRON	LILAC
CLARET	
COCOA	MAGENTA
CORDOVAN	MAHOGANY
CRIMSON	MAIZE
	MARIGOLD
DOVE	MAUVE
	MOSS
EBONY	
ECRU	OLIVE
EMERALD	

PINK	TEAL
POPPY	TITIAN
	TOPAZ
RAVEN	TURQUOISE
RED	
ROAN	UMBER
ROSE	
ROSY	VERMILION
RUBY	VIOLET
RUSSET	VIRIDIAN
SCARLET	WISTERIA
SIENNA	
SILVER	XANTHENE
SLATE	
STEEL	ZINC
STERLING	

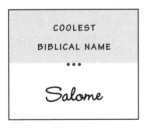

COOLEST
BIBLICAL NAME
• • •
Salome

Sonata

Music Names

I f it's true that music "has charms to soothe a savage breast" and is "the food of love," then it stands to reason that the words used to describe music would be charming and soothing, lyrical, rhythmic, and rousing. Some of them could make even make melodious baby names:

ADAGIO	BRIO
ALLEGRO	
ALTO	CADENCE
ARABESQUE	CADENZA
ARIA	CALLIOPE

CALYPSO	MADRIGAL
CANTATA	MALAGUENA
CAPPELLA	MANDOLIN
CAPRICE	MARIMBA
CARILLON	MELODY
CELLO	MINUET
CLARION	
	OPERA
DIVA	
DULCIMER	RAGA
	REED
ETUDE	RHYTHM
FIFER	SERAPHINE
FLAMENCO	SERENADE
	SONATA
HARMONY	SONATINA
HARP	SYMPHONY
JAZZ	TANGO
	TEMPO
LUTE	TIMPANI
LYRE	
LYRIC	VIOLA

Jupiter

Space Names

There are cool celebrity star names like Uma and Bono, and then there are the even more extreme astronomical star and constellation names, which might appeal to parents looking for something truly unique and celestial—in other words, a heavenly name. Some stellar ideas:

ADHARA	ALULA
ALCYONE	ALYA
ALIOTH	AMALTHEA
ALTAIR	ANDROMEDA

AQUILA	JANUS
ARA	JUPITER
ARIES	
ASCELLA	LEDA
ATLAS	LIBRA
ATRIA	LUNA
AURORA	
AZHA	MAIA
	MARS
BELLATRIX	MEISSA
	MERCURY
CAELUM	METEOR
CALLISTO	MIMOSA
CALYPSO	MIRA
CAPELLA	MOON
CASSIOPEIA	
CHARA	NASHIRA
COLUMBA	NAVI
	NOVA
ELARA	
ELECTRA	OBERON
	ORION
GALATEA	
	PERSEUS
HALLEY	
	RHEA
IO	
IZAR	

SABIK   TITANIA
SHAULA
STAR   VEGA
STELLA   VENUS

TALITHA   ZANIAH
THALASSA   ZOSMA

Early

Beyond-name Names

In our book *Beyond Jennifer & Jason, Madison & Montana*, we included vast numbers of word names, nature names, day names, and surname-names. While these names are, for the most part, undoubtedly cool, there are an uncountable number of them, beyond the scope of any one book. The only limits are your reference books, your imagination, and your taste. If you'd like to explore further in this territory on your own, we can direct you to *J & J, M & M* as well as to your dictionary, field guide, and phone book. To give you an idea of some of the selections from these categories, we offer here a few of the best:

AFTERNOON	JUNIPER
ARBOR	
	KEATON
BAY	
BEECH	LANE
BIRCH	LARK
BOGART	LINCOLN
CABOT	MADIGAN
CAMEO	MONDAY
CANYON	
CHRISTMAS	NORTH
CLARITY	NOVEMBER
DECEMBER	PIKE
EARLY	QUARRY
EASTER	
EDISON	SALMON
	SEASON
FINCH	SONNET
GRAYSON	TIERNEY
GROVE	
HALE	

Kool

Too-cool Names

Maybe you can't be too rich or too thin, but if you're a name, it just may be possible to be too cool.

What makes a name too cool? Trying so hard that coolness is its main—and maybe its only—merit. Being so aggressively hip that poor little Kool will bend under the expectations of grooviness created by his name. Sure, there are kids named Babe or Scorpio who grow into their names' images, but you're asking a lot of a child who, let's face it, is just as likely to have crooked teeth and a shyness issue as an awesome bod.

While the line of what constitutes a too-cool name seems to get redrawn every day, these choices will probably be on the wrong side of it for a long time to come.

ARMANI	MAVERICK
BABE	PORSCHE
BRANDY	PRINCE
BREEZE	
BUCK	RAMBO
	RIDER
CALIFORNIA	
CHEYENNE	SCORPIO
CONGO	SINBAD
CROCKETT	SUGAR
DESIREE	TALON
DUKE	THOR
	TIGER
FREE	
	VICE
HARLEY	VULCAN
KOOL	WILD

COOLEST

HERO NAME

• • •

Rudy

INDEX

Barzillai, 117
Bas, Basia, 48, 87
Basil, Basilia, Bazel, 15, 25, 112, 117, 122
Bathsheba, 31, 96
Beale, 100
Beata, Beatrice, Beatrix, 14, 23, 43, 51, 112, 126
Becan, 117
Bechet, Bechette, 67, 70, 87, 140
Beck, Becker, Beckett, 87, 93, 105
Beech, 163
Behan, 93
Beige, 155
Bella, Bellatrix, Belle, Bellezza, Bellow, 43, 70, 93, 121, 144, 160
Ben, Benjamin, Bennato, Benno, Benson, Benvolio, 12, 24, 39, 48, 60, 100, 103, 117, 144
Benajah, Benatar, 87, 122
Benecio, Benet, Benicia, Benicio, 18, 39, 56, 93, 117
Berlin, 27
Bernadette, Bernard, 116, 129
Bertha, Bertram, 129
Bessie, 87
Bethany, Bethia, 6, 14, 116, 119
Beulah, 129
Beyoncé, 56, 87
Bianca, Bianco, 6, 23, 144
Bibiana, 116
Bichette, 140
Bijou, 140
Bill, Billie, Wilbur, Wilfred, Wilhelm, Will, Willa, Willem, William, Wilma, Willow, Wills, 11–12, 24, 31, 33, 35, 45, 50–51, 73–74, 79, 85,

87, 95–101, 105, 130, 138
Bimini, 27
Bing, 87
Birch, 163
Bix, 87
Bizzy, 91
Bjergen, 60
Bjork, Bjorn, 56, 87, 105
Blake, 7, 83, 93, 136
Blanca, Blanche, 126, 148
Blase, 117
Bleu, Blu, Blue, 56, 70, 140, 144, 154
Bliss, 153
Bly, 93
Bo, Boaz, 39, 105, 117
Bogart, 163
Bohan, 83
Bolivia, 27
Bolton, 135
Bonanza, 60
Bono, 76, 87, 159
Bonté, 140
Boris, 105
Boston, 27
Bowie, 87
Bozrah, 119
Braden, Brady, Brayden, 7–8, 135
Brahms, 87
Branch, Brandon, Brandy, 6, 105, 138, 165
Braque, 83
Brasilia, Brason, Brazil, 27, 135
Braxon, 135
Breckin, 56
Bree, Briana, Brianna, Brin, Briony, Bryn, Bryony, 10, 14, 48, 96, 140
Breeze, 165
Brendan, Brent, 7, 136
Brett, 96
Brevin, 135
Brick, 100, 155

Bridget, Brigitte, 18, 48
Briley, 136
Brio, 144, 148, 157
Bristol, 27
Brogan, 117, 135
Brom, 100
Brontë, Bronwen, 14, 93
Brooklyn, Brooks, 6, 105
Brown, 155
Bruce, Bruno, Bryce, Brycen, Bryson, 7, 12, 39, 62, 79, 117, 136
Buck, 165
Buff, 155

Cab, Cabe, Cabot, 87, 135, 163
Cade, Cadeau, Caden, Cadena, Cadence, Cadenza, Caiden, Cayden, Kaden, Kadin, Kaiden, Kayden, 8, 135–36, 140, 144, 148, 157
Caelum, 160
Cain, Canela, Kain, Kane, 12, 65, 93, 148
Cairo, 27, 39, 80
Cal, Cala, Calah, Calais, Calder, Calia, Calico, California, Calista, Calla, Callaia, Callan, Calandra, Callas, Calliope, Callisto, Calloway, Callum, Calton, Calum, Calvin, Calvina, Kallan, 15, 18, 27, 34, 39, 45, 56, 82–83, 87, 106, 112, 119, 135, 144, 148, 157, 160, 165
Cale, Caleb, Caledonia, Kaleb, 6, 27, 45, 48, 70, 87, 117
Calypso, 39, 158, 160
Cam, Camden, Cameo, Cameron, Camilla, Campana, Camryn, 5,

Manfred, 24
Manon, 19
Manuela, 19
Manzu, 84
Mara, Marable, 113, 116
Marcel, Marcella,
   Marcellus, Marciana,
   Marco, Marcus,
   Marquis, 7, 19, 40, 81,
   106, 113–14
Mardi, 142
Marea, Marée, Marek,
   Marèna, Maria,
   Mariah, Marian,
   Marie, Mary, Mireille,
   Miriam, Mitzi, 5, 11,
   20, 23, 33, 50–51, 65,
   88, 113, 142, 146,
   150, 154
Margaret, Margay, 33,
   44, 48, 50, 98, 101,
   142
Marigold, Marimba,
   Marin, Marina,
   Marine, Marino,
   Marion, Maris,
   Mariska, Marisol,
   Marit, Marius, 19, 40,
   57, 84, 98, 101, 106,
   155, 158
Marley, 57, 88
Marron, Marrone, 142,
   146
Mars, Marshall, 125, 160
Martha, Martina, 23, 33,
   71, 106
Maso, Mason, Massimo,
   7, 40, 50, 76, 134, 146
Mateo, 20
Matilda, Matita, Matiz,
   127, 137, 146, 150
Matta, Matthias,
   Mattolina, 84, 118,
   146
Maude, 44
Maureen, Maurice,
   Maurus, Maury, 50,
   114, 125, 130
Mauve, Maverick, 142,
   155, 165

Max, Maximo,
   Maximus, Maxon,
   Maxwell, 8, 34, 62,
   66, 99, 114, 135
May, Maya, 5, 25, 44, 94,
   127
Mccarthy, Mccartney,
   37, 88
Mcdermott, 37
Mcelroy, 37
Mcenroe, 37, 106
Mcewan, 37, 94
Mcgrath, 37
Mckenna, Mackenzie,
   Mckenzie, Makenzie,
   4, 6, 36
Mckeon, 37
Mckinley, 37
Mcmanus, 37
Mcnally, 37
Mcneil, 37
Mcpherson, 37
Mehta, 88, 94
Meissa, 160
Mejilla, 150
Melanctha, 98
Melchior, 101
Melilot, Melisent, 113,
   142
Melody, 158
Melvin, 130
Memphis, 28, 76
Mena, Menas, 57, 114
Meraude, 113
Mercedes, Mercury,
   Mercy, 6, 11, 33, 76,
   160
Meriall, Merise, Merry,
   11, 113, 142
Mervyn, 130
Meteor, 160
Mia, Mya, Mies, 5, 14,
   84, 106
Miami, 28
Micah, Micajah,
   Michael, Michal,
   Michelle, Mickey,
   Miguel, Mikayla,
   Mike, Mikhail,
   Mikolas, ix, 4, 8, 12,

   20–21, 72, 78, 97,
   100, 105, 116, 118,
   122, 134
Mignon, 19
Milan, Milla, Millais,
   Millay, Millet, Millie,
   14, 25, 28, 57, 84, 94,
   137
Mildred, 129
Miles, Milo, xi, 12, 40,
   46, 76, 88, 101
Milton, 12, 130
Mimosa, 33, 160
Minerva, 113
Mingus, 81, 88
Minnie, 57
Minta, 137
Minuet, 158
Mira, Mirabelle, Miracle,
   Miranda, Mirando, 5,
   44, 142, 146, 150,
   153, 160
Miro, 75, 84
Mirtha, 62
Mitzi, 31
Miuccia, 84
Mo, Moe, Mos, Mos
   Def, Moses, xi, 35, 50,
   88, 91, 118
Modesty, 33
Moineau, 142
Moira, 14
Molly, 10, 25, 47
Monday, 163
Monet, 57, 84
Monique, 31
Monroe, 12
Montana, Montego,
   Montoya, Monty, 12,
   40, 106, 137
Moon, 57, 160
Moore, Mor, 84, 101
Morandi, 84
Moreau, 84
Morgan, Morgana, 5,
   12, 116, 146
Mori, Moriah, Morisot,
   84, 116
Morley, 125
Morocco, 28, 40

Presley, Preston, 8, 81, 88
Prima, Primo, Primrose,
    Primula, Primus, 33,
    41, 113–14, 147
Priscilla, 33, 116, 137
Pru, Prudence, 33, 51,
    121

Quebec, 28, 101
Quentin, Q, 16, 51, 118
Quincy, Quinn, Quinta,
    Quintana, Quintas,
    28, 46, 51, 88, 101,
    150

Rabanne, Raeburn, 84
Rachel, 33, 63
Rafe, Raffaela, Rafferty,
    Ralph, Raphael,
    Raphaela, 19, 35, 51,
    58, 67, 77, 84, 118
Rain, Rayne, 60, 63, 98,
    113
Raleigh, 28, 94
Ramon, Ramona,
    Ramone, Ramos, 21,
    31, 88, 135
Raoul, 12, 21
Raven, 6, 31, 156
Ray, Raymond, 12, 25,
    77, 88
Red, 156
Redmond, 16
Reece, Reese, Rhys, 16,
    58, 61, 69, 94, 107
Reed, 46, 158
Reina, Reine, 142, 150
Rem, Remi, Remy, 84,
    118, 137
Remember, 153
Remington, 84
Remus, 114
Renata, 19
Rence, 137
Renee-Therese, 138
Reno, 41, 150
Reo, Rio, 28, 41, 135
Reuben, Ruban, 118,
    142
Rex, 16

Reynold, 16
Rhea, Rheya, 62, 160
Rhett, 101
Rhiannon, 15
Rhonwen, 15
Rhythm, 158
Rian, 137
Rider, Ryder, 84, 165
Riella, 137
Riley, Rylee, 5, 7, 101,
    136
Rima, 98
Ring, 94
Rinoa, 65
Riona, 116
Ripley, 31
Riva, Rivage, 142, 147
Rivo, 147
Roald, 94
Roan, Roano, 77, 147,
    154, 156
Roark, 101
Robbia, Robin, xi, 16,
    84
Rocco, 41, 77
Roche, 142
Rodin, Rodion, 84, 101
Rodrigo, 41
Rogan, 135
Rohan, Rowan, 16
Roland, Rollo, 16, 41
Roma, Roman,
    Romanus, Romany,
    28, 114, 118
Romeo, 78, 101
Romola, 98
Romulus, 114
Ronald, Ronan, Ronde,
    12, 16, 107
Rooney, 12
Rory, 16
Rosalind, Rosamond,
    Rosanna, Rosario,
    Rose, Rosemary,
    Rosy, 11, 33, 44, 58,
    68, 73, 98, 121, 127,
    154, 156
Roux, 63, 142
Roxanne, Roxie, Roxy,
    31

Rubi, Ruby, 6, 10, 31,
    78, 150, 156
Rufus, 88, 101, 123
Rupert, 16, 118
Ruth, 33, 116, 127

Sabbia, Sabik, Sabina,
    Sabine, Sabio, Sabo,
    Sabra, Sabrina, 5, 98,
    107, 113, 143, 147,
    151, 161
Sade, 58, 89
Sadie, 4, 6, 31, 44, 51,
    67, 74, 77–78
Saffron, Safran, 11, 58,
    117, 143
Salinger, Salita, 95, 147
Salma, Salmon, 58, 61,
    63, 163
Salome, Salome Violetta,
    31, 78, 156
Sam, Samantha, Samara,
    Samaria, Samedi,
    Samoa, Samson,
    Samuel, Samus, 6, 11,
    28, 34, 61–62, 65, 72,
    118–19, 123, 143
Sanne, 19
Sansonnet, 143
Santana, Santiago, 89,
    102
Sapphira, 116
Sarai, Sarazen, 107,
    116
Sargent, 84
Sarita, 19
Saroyan, 95
Sasha, 44
Saskia, 11, 19
Satchell, 78
Satine, Satiné, 63, 143
Saul, 118
Savanna, Savannah,
    Savarin, 5, 10, 143
Savion, Savita, 19, 58
Sawyer, x, 102
Scala, 147
Scarlet, Scarlett, 32, 58,
    80, 98, 156
Schmally, 63

About the Authors

PAMELA REDMOND SATRAN is a contributing editor for *Parenting* magazine and a columnist for *BabyTalk*. Her first novel, *The Man I Should Have Married*, was published by Downtown Press/ Pocket Books in March 2003. Satran's articles appear frequently in publications ranging from the *New York Times* to *Glamour* and *Self*. She lives outside New York City with her husband and three children.

LINDA ROSENKRANTZ is the author of seven other books in addition to the baby-naming series, ranging from *Gone Hollywood,* a social history of the film colony; to a childhood memoir, *My Life as a List: 207 Things About My (Bronx) Childhood;* to her latest book, a history and anthology of telegrams. A resident of Los Angeles, she also writes a syndicated weekly column on collectibles.

As authorities on baby names, they have been quoted in *People,* the *Wall Street Journal,* and the *New York Times Magazine.* They have also made appearances on nationally syndicated shows such as *Oprah* and the CNN Morning News. Their baby-name books have sold nearly one million copies.